GLOBETROTTER™

Travel Guide

Mrs. M

AUSTRALIA

BRUCE ELDER

NEW HOLLAND

NEW
HOLLAND

★★★ Highly recommended
★★ Recommended
★ See if you can

Eighth edition published in 2010
by New Holland Publishers (UK) Ltd
London • Cape Town • Sydney • Auckland
10 9 8 7 6 5 4 3 2 1
website: www.newhollandpublishers.com

Garfield House, 86 Edgware Road
London W2 2EA, United Kingdom

80 McKenzie Street
Cape Town 8001, South Africa

Unit 1, 66 Gibbes Street, Chatswood
NSW 2067, Australia

218 Lake Road, Northcote,
Auckland, New Zealand

Distributed in the USA by
The Globe Pequot Press, Connecticut

This guidebook has been written by independent
authors and updaters. The information therein
represents their impartial opinion, and neither
they nor the publishers accept payment in return
for including in the book or writing more
favourable reviews of any of the establishments.
Whilst every effort has been made to ensure that
this guidebook is as accurate and up to date as
possible, please be aware that the facts quoted are
subject to change, particularly the price of food,
transport and accommodation. The Publisher
accepts no responsibility or liability for any loss,
injury or inconvenience incurred by readers or
travellers using this guide.

Publishing Manager: Thea Grobbelaar
DTP Cartographic Manager: Genené Hart
Editors: Carla Zietsman, Nicky Steenkamp,
Alicha van Reenen, Melany McCallum
Design and DTP: Nicole Bannister, Eloïse Moss
Cartographers: Reneé Spocter, Carryck Wise,
Genené Hart, Carl Germishuys

Reproduction by Resolution (Cape Town) and Hirt
& Carter (Pty) Ltd, Cape Town.
Printed and bound by Times Offset (M) Sdn. Bhd.,
Malaysia.

Keep us Current
Information in travel guides is apt to change,
which is why we regularly update our guides.
We'd be grateful to receive feedback if you've
noted something we should include in our
updates. If you have new information, please
share it with us by writing to the Publishing
Manager, Globetrotter, at the office nearest
to you (addresses on this page). The most
significant contribution to each new edition
will receive a free copy of the updated guide.

Photographic Credits:
Travel Pix Collection/awl-images.com: page 30;
Shaen Adey (NHIL), title page, pages 38, 41, 54,
57, 112, 117; **Murray Child**, page 49 (bottom);
Bruce Elder, pages 25, 40, 43, 49 (top), 56, 67,
88, 89 (top), 91, 104, 105, 110, 119; **Pictures
Colour Library**, cover, page 62; **Nick Rains**,
pages 4, 6, 8, 10, 11, 12, 13, 15, 17, 18, 19, 22,
24, 27, 28, 33, 34, 36, 42, 46, 52, 55 (top and
bottom), 89 (bottom), 108, 111, 114, 118, 119
(bottom); **Ken Stepnell**, pages 7, 9, 60, 64, 66,
68, 72, 75 (top and bottom), 79, 80, 85, 86, 90,
93, 97, 99, 102 (top and bottom), 103.
NHIL = New Holland Image Library

Front Cover: The 'Three Sisters' Blue Mountains,
Katoomba, NSW Australia.
Title Page: The Pinnacles, Nambung National
Park, Western Australia.

CONTENTS

NEXT 96 km

1
Introducing Australia

Australia is a country of remarkable diversity. It ranges across more than 30° of latitude from the tropics of north **Queensland**, the **Northern Territory** and northern **Western Australia** through to the temperate rainforests of southern **Tasmania**. The great appeal of Australia, with the exception of cool, moist Tasmania which defies every generalisation about the country, is the vastness of the landscape, the extent of the desert areas (it has the second-largest dry desert area in the world after the Sahara), the incredibly blue skies and its richly multicultural society.

Australia enjoys long periods of **sunny, dry weather** and consequently is essentially an outdoor society characterised by informality, egalitarianism, friendliness and a genuine dislike of protocol and pretentiousness.

The strengths of modern Australia lie in the acceptance that this is a country where life is easy, where the narrow social stratification that is so much a part of European society has been abandoned.

Look at Australia on the weekend and you will find sport ovals full and beaches crowded. Watch the main arteries out of any major city on a Friday afternoon and you will find them choked with cars full of bushwalkers, people travelling to their holiday homes, surfers, fishermen and people fleeing the cities. However, it should always be remembered that, although Australians still love the idea of the rural 'bronzed Aussie', less than 15% of the population actually live in rural areas, or 'the bush' as it is called.

TOP ATTRACTIONS

*** Great Barrier Reef: magnificent coral formations and exotic marine life.
*** Uluru and Kata Tjuta: spectacular rock remnants surrounded by desert. Best seen at dawn and dusk.
*** Sydney: the beautiful harbour setting, Bridge and Opera House are some of the city's premier attractions.
*** Great Ocean Road: dramatic and impressive coastal scenery against a backdrop of rural peacefulness.

Opposite: *Signs warn travellers to watch out for camels, wombats and kangaroos as they travel through the 'outback'.*

FACTS AND FIGURES

- **World's largest electorate:** Kalgoorlie, Western Australia, covers over 2,000,000km² (770,000 sq miles).
- **Largest property:** Anna Creek Station in South Australia is the world's largest pastoral lease. Covering over 30,100km² (nearly six million acres) it is bigger than Belgium and half the size of England.
- **Largest basin:** the Great Artesian Basin covering 1,700,000km² (650,000 sq miles).
- **Tallest building:** Q1 on Queensland's Gold Coast is Australia's tallest residential building and, apart from navigation towers in Western Australia and Victoria, the tallest building in the country.

Below: *The Australian passion for the beach, sport and surfing is expressed in the volunteer surf life-savers who test their skills against the ocean breakers and protect the people who come to surf and relax each weekend.*

Far removed from the pains and sufferings of the rest of the world, Australia is fast becoming the **middle-class paradise** that the people of Europe have dreamt about for centuries.

Visitors to Australia will be confronted by a continent of bewildering diversity. They can experience the tropical magic of the **Great Barrier Reef** with its fantastic coral formations and the vastness of the **Great Artesian Basin** which runs down the centre of the country – an area where steaming bores bring water to the parched land from hundreds of metres below the earth's surface.

They can marvel at the beauty and elegance of the modern cities and wonder at how they can travel for hundreds of kilometres without ever seeing another human being.

In Tasmania they can be seduced by wild beaches where waves, uninterrupted by land since they left South America, crash onto lonely shores, and they can marvel at the dramatic glaciation of the island's cold and forbidding **Cradle Mountain** area, which stands in sharp contrast to the red deserts of the mainland.

Beyond these features there is the gently undulating cattle country between the Great Dividing Range and the Pacific Ocean, the beauty of the **Snowy Mountains** in winter, the vast plains where sheep and wheat sustain small rural communities, the dramatic red soils and beaches of the Kimberley and the huge jarrah and karri trees on the southwestern tip of Western Australia.

But no journey around Australia, and no one wanting to understand this mysterious continent, should miss the '**dead heart**'. **Alice Springs** with its dry Todd River and the MacDonnell Range stretching east and west of the town; **Uluru**, 'the greatest stone on Earth', always marvellous at dusk and dawn; the huge outcrops that are Kata Tjuta; and the jagged canyons – **Standley Chasm**, **Simpson's Gap**, **Kings Canyon** – are all places seemingly designed by nature simply for the purpose of taking the visitor's breath away.

Left: *Towering above Dove Lake are the jagged, snow-capped peaks of Cradle Mountain. Cradle Mountain–Lake St Clair National Park is one of Tasmania's premier tourist destinations.*

THE LAND
The Oldest Continent

Many regard Australia as the oldest continent on earth. Certainly it seems to be both the most stable and the most eroded of the continents. Geologists have dated parts of the Western Australian shield at 3000 million years old.

Hundreds of millions of years ago, there was a mountain range in central Australia which was higher than Mount Everest. When travellers arrive at **Ellery Creek Big Hole**, one of the many gorges and chasms which split the MacDonnell Range, they will see a notice board near the car park which explains that 'All around you there is evidence of a great mountain-building episode in the formation of Central Australia. You can see tortured folds of rock which formed deep in the earth and when great heat and pressure pushed up 10,000m (33,000ft) of mountains . . . 350 million years of erosion have almost worn them away, exposing the deeper folded rocks'. It is at moments like this that the traveller realises how ancient the continent really is.

> ### THE FLAT CONTINENT
>
> Australia is the lowest and flattest continent on earth. Only six per cent has an elevation above 700m (2300ft) and the country's highest mountain, Mount Kosciuszko, is only 2229m (7300ft) above sea level. It is scarcely more than a substantial hill and can be reached in an easy day's hike. The continent's largest flat surface is the Nullarbor Plain which covers over 250,000km^2 (100,000 sq miles).

Above: *Lying to the north of Uluru (Ayers Rock) are 36 smaller monoliths known as Kata Tjuta (the Olgas). It is thought that Kata Tjuta may have once been many times the size of Uluru.*

To understand the physical shape of Australia it is best to think in terms of **four distinct regions**. Along the east coast (where most of the country's population lives) there is an upland region known as the **Great Dividing Range**. This is a series of plateaux, high plains and spectacular gorges, which run from **Cape York** in northern Queensland to the southern tip of **Tasmania**. Between here and the Pacific Ocean is the most productive land, enjoying good rainfall and moderate temperatures.

Beyond the Great Dividing Range are the **Murray**, **Eyre** and **Carpentaria basins,** which stretch from the **Gulf of Carpentaria** in northern Queensland through western **New South Wales** into western **Victoria** and parts of **South Australia**. This is the region that early European explorers thought was a huge inland sea because the major river systems, instead of running to the east, run in a south-westerly direction, either reaching Lake Eyre or joining the Murray–Darling basin and flowing into the Southern Ocean at Lake Alexandrina.

Over half of Australia is taken up by the vast **Western Craton**, a series of low-lying plateaux and desert regions which extend from the Barkly Tablelands of the Northern Territory across to the Kimberley and Pilbara through the vast desert regions of the **Great Victoria Desert, Gibson Desert** and **Great Sandy Desert**. This is a region characterised by seemingly endless ridges of sand dunes (from the air much of the area looks like an uninhabited piece of corrugated iron) and almost blood-red soil which is rich in iron-ore. This is where nature, over millions of years, has eroded all the major formations – with the notable exceptions of **Uluru**, the **MacDonnell Range** and the strange formations of the **Kimberley** region in Western Australia.

Seas and Shores

Australia is justifiably famous for its coastline. Although it is a country which is almost exactly the same size as USA (excluding Alaska), most of the population live at or near the coast. More than half the towns in the country are located in New South Wales and Victoria and over 80% of the population live in the narrow coastal strip from Cairns in north Queensland through to Adelaide.

There is considerable diversity in this coastline but there is little doubt that the most impressive feature is the **Great Barrier Reef**. It can be seen from the moon and, as every *Trivial Pursuit* buff knows, it is the largest structure on earth built by living creatures.

The opportunity to explore the Reef by pleasure craft, snorkelling or diving is an opportunity to explore a wonderland of exotic fish and magical coral formations.

From Bundaberg through to the north of Victoria the coast is characterised by excellent swimming and surfing beaches (some have international reputations for the quality of their waves) set between low-lying headlands which are popular haunts for fishermen. These conditions continue into South Australia and around much of the coast of Tasmania. At particular points, notably along the **Great Ocean Road** in Victoria and along the west coast of Tasmania, the beaches give way to rugged cliffs and spectacular scenery.

Most of the coast has good facilities for mooring fishing boats and pleasure craft and, where necessary, the local communities have constructed breakwaters and wharves.

Beyond Eyre Peninsula in South Australia lie the dramatic cliffs which fall sheer to the sea at the edge of the **Nullarbor Plain**. It is not until Western Australia that the cliffs again give way to beaches and harbours. One of the country's best kept secrets is the coastline from Esperance to Albany and around to Busselton and Perth. Characterised by breathtakingly white sands and stunning granite headlands, this coastline is arguably the most beautiful in the whole country. Only isolation and the cold winds from the Southern Ocean have protected it from development.

Above: *The northeastern coast of Victoria is famous for the vast Ninety Mile Beach. A popular spot for quiet holidays, the long beach offers surf fishers excellent opportunities to catch an evening meal.*

GREAT BARRIER REEF

The Great Barrier Reef is Australia's most awe-inspiring natural wonder. Its coral formations, the diversity of the tropical fish which live in the area, and the fact that it is largely untouched by the modern world make it a natural magnet for visitors. The Reef extends south from the coast of Papua New Guinea for over 2000km (1242 miles) to Lady Elliot Island near Bundaberg, Queensland. Divided by scientists into northern, central and southern regions it is in fact an interconnecting series of some 2000 individual reefs and 71 coral islands, featuring over 400 varieties of coral and 1500 types of fish.

The coastline of Western Australia has many beautiful
beaches and is noted for its excellent fishing. Of particular
note is **Shark Bay** with its famous friendly dolphins at
Monkey Mia and the glorious beaches around Broome.

Beyond Broome, around the northern coastline to
Cairns and the Barrier Reef, the waters are characterised
by mangrove swamps, broad estuaries from the rivers
which are swollen by the rains from 'the wet' which
sweeps across the coast every summer, and the ever-
present dangers of crocodiles, sharks, deadly jellyfish
and stingrays.

Climate

Australia is a dry continent. Over two-thirds of the
country experiences rainfall of less than 500mm (20in) per
annum and more than one-third of the continent (mainly
from the centre across into Western Australia) has an
annual rainfall of less than 250mm (10in).

However, it is important to recognise that Australia is
not just one vast desert. The areas of greatest population
– along the eastern coastline and in the southwestern
corner of Western Australia – typically receive rainfall
over 1000mm (40in), substantial snowfalls occur during
winter (June to August) in Tasmania and on the Snowy

Right: *The MacDonnell
Range, which stretches to
the east and west of Alice
Springs, is cut by a
number of gorges offering
a cool respite from the
desert heat. Glen Helen,
lying 133km (83 miles)
west of 'the Alice', is
noted for its exceptional
tranquillity and beauty.*

Mountains (which stretch from southern New South Wales into northern Victoria), and the northern coastline experiences tropical conditions including monsoonal rainfall above 1500mm (60in) and long periods of humid summer weather. Australia lies between the latitudes of 10°41'S and 43°39'S and consequently any generalisations about the climate are very difficult.

It is worth remembering the extremes of the country's temperatures. There was a summer (1923) when the town of Marble Bar in Western Australia recorded temperatures which never dropped below 37.8°C (100°F) for 161 consecutive days.

The period before 'the wet' (December to March) in places like Katherine and Darwin rivals anywhere in the world's tropical zones for heat and humidity and, when the weather is right, the Snowy Mountains have more substantial snowfields than Switzerland.

Above: *The tiny mining town of Marble Bar in Western Australia is known as 'the hottest town in Australia'. During all the time that records have been kept the temperature at the town has never dropped below 0°C (32°F).*

Right: *A sudden storm will turn Australia's deserts into oceans of coloured flowers, but nothing compares to the red and black flowers of Sturt's desert pea.*

Opposite top: *Kangaroos rest during the day, but at dawn and dusk it is quite common to see them in outback Australia.*

Opposite bottom: *The Australian deserts are full of extraordinary animals. The thorny devil lives on small black ants and has been known to eat over 1000 ants in a single sitting.*

Plant Life

The enduring image of Australia is the eucalypt or 'gum tree' which is found wherever there is adequate rainfall and the land has not been cleared. In its most beautiful manifestation, particularly in the Blue Mountains to the west of Sydney, the eucalypt forest gives the appearance of being lightly brushed with a smoky blue.

It has been estimated that Australia has some 20,000 species of flora which range from the tropical rainforests through mangroves, sclerophyll forests, savannas, mallee scrub and desert. The desert, particularly after rain, is spectacular with the sharp red and black of Sturt's desert pea, which is typical of this harsh beauty.

The best way to appreciate the richness and diversity of Australia's flora is to visit Western Australia when the bush is in bloom. To the north and east of Perth there are literally hundreds of kilometres of bush which come alive with native plants.

Animals

Isolated from Southeast Asia, Australia has developed its own, unique fauna. Animals such as the platypus and echidna (both egg-laying mammals) and the marsupials – kangaroos, wallabies, wombats, koalas, numbats and phalangers – have given Australia a reputation as a

LOOKING FOR ANIMALS

Australia has some famously unique animals – the kangaroo, platypus and the koala which can be seen in Queensland at the **Lone Pine Koala Sanctuary**, Brisbane; the **Australia Zoo** run by Terri Irwin, the wife of the late Crocodile Hunter, Steve Irwin; **Currumbin Sanctuary**, the **Cairns Tropical Zoo**, Cairns. In New South Wales they can be seen at **Taronga Park Zoo** and **Featherdale Wildlife Park**, Sydney; **Symbio Wildlife Sanctuary**, Helensburgh; and **Western Plains Zoo**, Dubbo.

LOOKING FOR ANIMALS

Native animal sanctuaries and zoos in Victoria include the **Royal Melbourne Zoo** and **Healesville Sanctuary**. In Tasmania the most famous animal sanctuary is the **Tasmanian Devil Park** at Taranna. Sanctuaries in South Australia include the **Cleland Wildlife Park** at Mt Lofty, **Warrawong Sanctuary** at Mylor and the **Adelaide Zoo**. In Western Australia the zoos and sanctuaries include **Perth Zoo** and the **Caversham Wildlife Park**, Perth and **Underwater World**, Perth. **Rottnest Island**, **Penguin Island** and **Monkey Mia** are also famous wildlife watching destinations, and in the Northern Territory there are both **Territory Wildlife Park** at Berry Springs and **Kakadu National Park**.

country with strange and exotic animals. Indeed, when a dead specimen of platypus was sent to England by early settlers it was thought to be a hoax – a duck's bill attached to an unknown mammal.

Travelling through western New South Wales and western Queensland it is common to be confronted, particularly at dusk, by kangaroos leaping across the road.

There seems to be a popular perception that Australia is a country full of dangerous creatures – deadly redback and funnel-web spiders, large numbers of poisonous snakes, seas full of sharks, stonefish, sea snakes and deadly jellyfish, and rivers with crocodiles waiting for the unsuspecting swimmer. While this is not entirely accurate, it does pay to be careful.

In fact, Australia, with the exception of the dingo, has no large land-based carnivores. Consequently, a large number of land-based animals, with no mechanisms to protect themselves against predators, have developed on the continent. As a result, many native birds and small mammals have been devastated by introduced species – notably feral varieties of domestic dogs and cats. Similarly, the consumption of grass by grazing animals and introduced rabbits has placed enormous pressures on the kangaroo and wallaby populations.

Opposite: *Purnululu (Bungle Bungles) are one of the wonders of outback Western Australia. Formed over 350 million years ago, they have the appearance of gigantic bell-shaped rock towers with horizontal banding produced by layers of black lichens and orange silica.*

HISTORY IN BRIEF

The human history of Australia probably started around 65,000 years ago. There is considerable evidence that, at this time, the sea level was 120m (395 ft) lower than it is today, making the journey of the ancestors of Australia's Aboriginal people down through the Indonesian archipelago relatively easy.

Although archaeologists are constantly revising the date of the first settlement of the continent there is evidence that Aborigines were established as far south as the Perth area around 38,000 years ago. The important archaeological site at Lake Mungo in far western New South Wales has provided evidence that from 32,000 years ago Aborigines were living in that area and were using stone tools, engaging in ritual cremation, using ochre and eating the crustaceans which lived in the rivers and lakes in the area.

By 25,000 years ago Aborigines had moved into Tasmania. Throughout the country they were painting, hunting marsupials, grinding seeds and mining flint. This culture continued until Europeans arrived and settled at Port Jackson in 1788.

The Early Explorers

It is difficult to determine when the first non-Aborigines made contact with the continent. There is some evidence that the Chinese knew of the existence of a southern continent as early as the 13th century and it seems that the great Chinese explorer **Cheng Ho** reached the shores near modern-day Darwin sometime in the early 15th century.

It wasn't until the 16th century that Europeans began to acknowledge the existence of a southern continent. In 1531, a French cartographer put the name Terra Australis on a world map and by 1597, European maps were showing Australia as being separate from Papua New Guinea.

In 1606, the Dutch explorer **Willem Jansz** explored the western coast of Cape York and the Portuguese **Luis Vaez de Torres** sailed between Australia and Papua New Guinea. A decade later, **Dirck Hartog** sighted the northwest coast of Australia and left a pewter plate on an island near Shark Bay in Western Australia.

ABORIGINAL MUSIC

The **didgeridoo** is an Aboriginal wind instrument which produces a deep, rich, resonant sound. It is a wooden pipe about 2m (6ft) long and 5cm (2in) in diameter. Complex rhythmic patterns are played using breathing techniques which allow for continuous sound.Didgeridoos are traditionally used in tribal ceremonies called **corroborees** in which spiritual, festive or war-like intentions are expressed through rituals of music and dance.

For the next 150 years explorers continued to investigate the coast. The most significant were **Abel Tasman** who reached Tasmania (which he called Van Diemen's Land) in November 1642, and **William Dampier** who explored the coast of Western Australia in 1699.

However, all these explorations and discoveries became insignificant when **Captain James Cook**, having observed the transit of Venus in Tahiti, sailed the barque HM *Endeavour* west and reached Point Hicks on 20 April 1770. Cook sailed along the east coast of Australia and it was on his recommendation that **Captain Arthur Phillip** sailed the brig HMS *Supply* into Botany Bay (now part of metropolitan Sydney), arriving on 18 January 1788. A week later he moved north to the magnificent natural mooring at Port Jackson where he established a convict colony. This was the beginning of European settlement in Australia.

Convicts and Explorers

Australia's European origins were founded in unfortunate circumstances. Following the loss of their American colonies in 1783, the British had decided to establish a penal colony at **Botany Bay**. On board the First Fleet were some 730 convicts (about 570 men and 160 women), 250 free citizens (including many hard-drinking soldiers) and enough plants and livestock to establish a colony.

THE EARLY STRUGGLE

The 11 ships of the First Fleet sailed into Botany Bay on 18 January 1788. Captain Phillip was disappointed with the land and sent scouts north to Port Jackson. The settlement struggled in the early years. Convicts who had often received lengthy sentences for petty theft were not enthusiastic workers. The arrival of the second fleet in 1790 eased the struggle but starvation threatened the colony. It was not until 1808 that the first shipment of wool was sent to England.

HISTORICAL CALENDAR

c.60–68 000 BC Australian Aborigines settle continent.
1606 Willem Jansz is the first European to land on Australia.
1770 Captain Cook charts the east coast.
1788 Penal colony established around present-day Sydney.
1808 The Rum Rebellion (Governor Bligh deposed).
1813 Blue Mountains crossed.
1835 Melbourne founded.
1840 Convict transportation to NSW abolished.
1851 Gold rush begins.
1854 The Eureka Stockade.
1876 The last full-blooded Tasmanian Aborigine dies.
1880 Bushranger Ned Kelly captured and executed.
1901 Federation of the states and national independence.
1902 Women get federal vote.

1908 Canberra chosen as site for national capital.
1915 Gallipoli becomes site of tragic World War I campaign.
1942 Darwin and Sydney attacked by Japanese.
1947 International immigration drive begins.
1960 Aborigines granted citizenship (and the vote in 1962).
1972 Troops withdrawn from Vietnam after demonstrations.
1972 White Australia Policy formally ended.
1975 Prime Minister Whitlam sacked by Governor General.
1980 Azaria Chamberlain's disappearance leads to imprisonment of her mother – charges eventually quashed.
1993 Mabo ruling opens door to Aboriginal land claims.
1996 John Howard becomes

new Liberal PM.
2000 Sydney hosts the 2000 Olympic Games.
2001 Australia celebrates the Centenary of Federation. The country's 100th Birthday.
2003 Australia supports USA and Britain and goes to war against Iraq.
2004 John Howard becomes Australia's second longest-serving prime minister.
2005 International mineral boom sees BHP Billiton post a record breaking $8.5 billion annual profit.
2007 Australian population reaches 21 million.
2008 Kevin Rudd wins Federal election for ALP; John Howard becomes second sitting PM to lose seat in Federal election.

DISCOVERIES AND SETTLEMENTS

European Discoveries
1642 – Van Dieman's Land (Tasmania)
1770 – Botany Bay
1774 – Norfolk Island
1788 – Lord Howe Island
1802 – Spencer Gulf and St Vincent Gulf
1819 – Port Essington
1828 – Fremantle
1839 – Port Darwin

European Settlement Dates
1788 – Port Jackson (Sydney)
1804 – Newcastle and Hobart
1825 – Brisbane
1829 – Swan River (Perth)
1835 – Melbourne

Australia's history from 1788 until 1851 is the story of penal colonies and the development of a European society based on cheap labour and land conquests.

Once the convict settlement was established in Sydney there was a desire to explore and exploit the land. Within months, explorers had covered the entire Sydney basin and were seeking ways to cross the **Blue Mountains** to the west and find new pastures for sheep and cattle. Finally, in 1813, **Blaxland**, **Wentworth** and **Lawson** crossed the Blue Mountains and in the period up to 1840 explorers travelled west from Sydney across to South Australia (**Sturt**), south across the Snowy Mountains to the modern-day site of Melbourne (**Hume and Hovell**), north to modern-day Queensland (**Cunningham**) and west to the edges of the desert (**Sturt and Mitchell**).

By 1830, there were some 58,000 convicts in Australia. Many of them, after serving out the time of their sentences, stayed on and acquired land. It was not an easy society. The settlers moved out from the coastal settlements and grabbed any good land they could find. They treated the indigenous Aborigines like animals, thinking nothing of shooting and poisoning if the local population resisted the inexorable advance of western 'civilisation'.

By 1850, the original colony had been divided into five territorial divisions. From 1788 to 1824, New South Wales and Van Diemen's Land covered the eastern half of the country and the remaining area was unattached. In 1825, the original colony was extended to 129° longitude and in 1829, the rest of the continent became Western Australia when Perth was settled. In 1836, South Australia was proclaimed a free colony and in 1851 Victoria gained its independence from New South Wales. The final major change occurred when Queensland separated from New South Wales in 1859. During this time, the continent was extensively explored, with settlers and adventurers penetrating the interior and discovering vast tracts of excellent grazing land which led to rapid settlement of the region beyond the Great Dividing Range.

The Discovery of Gold

The society changed dramatically in 1851 with the discovery of gold in New South Wales. This was followed by further discoveries in Victoria, Western Australia and Queensland. It was during this time that Sydney and Melbourne became booming metropolitan areas buoyed by the wealth which poured into them from the goldfields.

The impact the Victorian gold rushes had on the state was remarkable. Rural labourers simply downed tools and headed for the goldfields. Transportation and tools were sold at exorbitant rates. Ships from Europe, Asia and the goldfields of California brought tens of thousands of prospectors to the state causing the population to increase from 80,000 in 1851 to 300,000 three years later.

Once the flurry of activity from the gold rushes had subsided the country settled down and in the late 19th century the wealth of the goldfields began to convert itself into vast riches derived from sheep, cattle and wheat industries, the development of other industries and the discovery of minerals other than gold.

Above: *In recent times, cruising down the Darling River has become a popular holiday trip and an opportunity to experience what was once a vital form of 19th-century transport.*

Veteran Californian goldminer, Edward Hargraves, first discovered gold near Bathurst in NSW in February 1851. This was quickly followed by gold strikes in Victoria, particularly at Ballarat, one of the largest-ever discoveries. Hopefuls soon poured into the new goldfields from Australia, China, Ireland, North America, England and Europe, although violent opposition to the Chinese sparked race riots. As a result, the population of Victoria increased dramatically and Melbourne rapidly became the largest and wealthiest city in Australia. The gold rushes continued until the end of the century with major discoveries in Western Australia and Queensland in the 1870s and 1880s.

Since 1933, the Australian census form has made it clear that answers to religious affiliation are not obligatory. In the 2006 census 18.7% of respondents said they had no religion and a total of 30.6% either refused to answer or said they had no religion. 63.9% declared themselves Christian, down from 86.2% in 1971 and 68% in 2001. Of these, 25.8% were Roman Catholic, 18.7% said they were Anglican and 2.7% were Orthodox. 5.7% indicated they belonged to the Uniting Church while, of the non-Christians, 2.1% were Buddhist, 1.7% Muslim 0.7% Hindu and 0.4% Jewish.

Below: *The image of Australia as a land of hardy rural workers persists. This sheep mustering is taking place in the New England ranges in northern New South Wales.*

Federation

For at least a decade prior to 1 January 1901, politicians argued the merits of federation. The states had developed their own laws and government procedures and they were unwilling to forsake these powers for some poorly understood concept of a federation which would represent all of Australia. However, the new Commonwealth Parliament was formally opened in Melbourne in 1901 and the seat of power was eventually moved to Canberra. The site had been chosen as early as 1908, but it was not until 1927 that the Federal Parliament began to sit regularly in the newly created city of Canberra.

The 20th Century

The history of Australia in the 20th century has been a mixture of huge success with the production and international sale of primary products, the deep scars left by two World Wars and the Vietnam war, the debate over a national identity and culture, and the emergence of the country as a significant force in the British Commonwealth and the Southeast Asia and Pacific regions.

Federation may have occurred in 1901, but the disparate group of states really had no common identity. It is worth remembering that, without modern transport, the people in Perth and Sydney were weeks away from each other and, apart from a common Anglo-Saxon background, had little in common. They were as far apart as London was from Athens.

The great defining moment for Australia and the Australian character occurred on 25 April 1915, when a brigade of the AIF (Australian Imperial Force) landed at Anzac Cove, Gallipoli. Nine months later troops were evacuated, but 7,594 Australians had been killed and another 19,500 wounded. It had been a disastrous campaign but the image of the brave, bronzed Australian prepared to fight against the odds and to laugh at authority had been born.

Left: *The Blue Mountains to the west of Sydney have spectacular views, delightful bushwalks and intimate waterfalls such as these in the Valley of the Waters.*

The courage Australian soldiers showed in World War I was once again in evidence in World War II, but this time not only were they fighting in Europe and North Africa but also to protect their own country from invasion by Japanese forces which had island-hopped from Japan to the Philippines, Singapore and the Dutch East Indies, and were carrying out bombing raids on the northern coastline and pushing down through Papua New Guinea.

The fear of invasion, partly produced by the vast empty areas of the continent and the rather simple notion that millions of people from Asia would slide down the map and arrive at the northern coast, dictated Australia's foreign policy until the 1980s.

This policy was largely responsible for Australia's involvement in the Korean and Vietnam wars, the country's willing alliance with the USA, and the belief that there was a need to be eternally vigilant.

Modern Multicultural Australia

It has only been in the last few decades that Australia, which until the 1950s was an entirely Anglo-Saxon culture imposed upon a local indigenous population, has started to become multicultural.

The arrival of over a million Italians and a million Greeks in the 20 years after World War II and, more recently, of many Asian people has helped to change attitudes and greatly improve the rather dour British cuisine which dominated throughout the country. The recognition that the world to the north of Australia was

MULTICULTURAL AUSTRALIA

As a result of the progressive removal of immigration restrictions based on race, colour and country of origin, plus the extension to non-British groups and refugees of assisted migration schemes, immigration rates greatly increased in the years after World War II, reaching a peak of 185,000 in 1969–70. After that there was a steady decline to a low of 53,000 in 1975–76, then it began to increase again. Migration increased in 2007–08 when 158,630 people migrated to Australia. In 2007–08 a total of 107,662 people became Australian citizens. Of those the top ten nationalities were British (27,369), Indian (9053), Chinese (8402), New Zealanders (6806), South African (5490), Iraqi (4216), Filipino (3827), Afghani (3174), Sudanese (3017) and Sri Lankan (2921).

- The birth rate in Australia is 12.8 per 1000 (world average 20.3) and the death rate 6.5 (world average 8.6) (2006 figures).
- The life expectancy for men is 78.5 years and 83.3 for women. Heart disease is the major cause of death followed by cancer.
- Of those aged 15 and over, 48.5% have not completed secondary education, while 14.2% have completed university.
- The average working week is 33.2 hours and the average weekly adult full-time earnings in February 2009 reached $1230.50.
- In 2006, 99.9% of houses have a refrigerator, 41.5% have a dishwasher, 96.4% have a washing machine and 544 in every 1000 have an automobile.

likely to become the economic engine room of the 21st century, made the country aware that it was the only European country in Asia.

As a result, Australia has become a much more interesting and exciting country than it was 50 years ago. It is diverse, multicultural, and eager to face new challenges and opportunities. It is, by most measures, an affluent and successful society.

GOVERNMENT AND ECONOMY

Although the last decade has seen a growing interest in Australia becoming a republic, the country is still a federal parliamentary state presided over by a **constitutional monarchy**. What this means, in practical terms, is that the government and legal system of the country is closely modelled on the British form of government and that Australia still has the British monarch as the head of state.

Each state has a **governor** who is the British monarch's official representative and whose primary functions, apart from attending numerous formal occasions, are to open parliament, to swear-in ministries, and to sign legislation into law. The federal equivalent is the **governor general**. Although generally regarded as a symbolic role (similar in status to the British monarch) all Australians recall the events of 1975, when the governor general of the time, **Sir John Kerr**, sacked Prime Minister **Gough Whitlam** and his government. This exercise of power was an exceptional event which caused considerable controversy. It is unlikely that such action will be taken again.

Australia has three tiers of government: federal, state and local. In practical terms, this division means that the **federal government** is concerned with national issues and thus is in charge of the military forces, aviation, diplomatic relations with other countries, national health policies, taxation, customs, industry, transport and communications, trade, resources, social security and similar areas of legislation and jurisdiction. The federal parliament, like its British blueprint, is divided into an upper house (**the Senate**) and a lower house (**the House of Representatives**).

The Senate was originally created to give equal representation to the states. Thus, although there are huge population discrepancies between, say, New South Wales and Tasmania, both states are represented by 12 elected members. In recent times, the Northern Territory and the Australian Capital Territory have each been represented by two Senate members. Senators are elected for six-year terms.

The primary function of the Senate, like the House of Lords, is that of a house of review. It critically evaluates legislation from the House of Representatives and makes suggestions and amendments. In recent times it has been difficult for either of the country's major political parties – the **Australian Labor Party** and the **Liberal Party of Australia** – to achieve an absolute majority in the Senate. This has meant that minority parties have been major forces in policy creation.

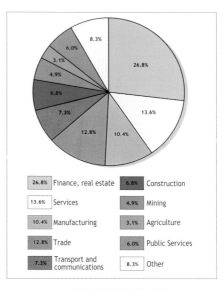

2005–06 GDP FIGURES

In spite of the importance of the Senate, the House of Representatives is still the engine room of federal politics. The **prime minister** is a member of the House of Representatives and, because each member is chosen from electorates which are roughly equal in their number of voters, there is a belief that this is the house which truly represents the wishes of Australians. The House of Representatives is re-elected every three years although it is the prime minister's prerogative to call an election.

Each state has a similar bicameral arrangement. The notable exception is Queensland, where the Upper House was abandoned, reflecting the widely held perception that, at state government level, the Upper House is a rather attractive sinecure for political worthies and has little effective power.

There are significant variations in voting behaviour and legislative process between states. However, the most com-

By 1947, 90.2% of the population was born in Australia, up from 77.1% in 1900. A further 7.7% were born in New Zealand or the UK. Australia's immigrant population has remained at around 23% of the nation's total population for the past decade. In 2006, 5.2% (a drop from 7.1% 15 years earlier) of Australians had been born in the UK and Ireland. 10.5% (down from 13.8% in 1992) had been born in Europe; and 7.3% were born in Asia and the Middle East; 2.0% in New Zealand and 9.3% in Africa, the Americas and elsewhere.

• In 2005–6 the Australian government's revenue was $A225,513 million and the expenditure was $A209,797 million.

• 91.6% of revenue was from taxation (50.7% personal income tax, 21.7% corporate tax, 15.3% excise and sales tax).

• 41.2% of expenditure was on social security and welfare; 17.9% on health; 7.5% on defence; 7.3% on public services; 8.0% on economic services; 7.9% on education; 2.6% interest on public debt and 7.6% on other services.

mon arrangement is for elections to be called every three years. The government is then constituted from the party with the largest number of representatives.

State governments are primarily concerned with state issues. Their major areas of legislative and administrative interest are education, the police force, roads, hospitals and local health.

The most grassroots of all the political forms is **local government**. There are thousands of local councils throughout Australia. Most are run by councillors who receive a small stipend and who make decisions about local roads, sewerage, rubbish collection, planning permission and property development in the local district. They are often constrained by state and federal legislation but they do enjoy considerable power within their local community.

The Economy

Over the past decade Australia has become a major supplier of raw materials (particularly coal and steel) to both China and India. This, combined with sound economic management, meant that by 2008 the country was uniquely placed to avoid the global financial collapse of 2008–09. In fact it became one of the very few western industrialised countries not to slip into recession, and the

huge economic downturn, while affecting unemployment and the general health of the economy, had a relatively minor impact on Australia. By 2005–06 the country's exports totalled $A151,792 million. This trade comprised 24.9% mineral fuels, 8.2% iron ore and 6.9% aluminium and aluminium ore. It was no accident that Japan accounted for 19.4% of the country's export trade followed by China with 13.6% and South Korea with 7.8%. The UK, a traditional trading partner, accounted for a mere 3.7% of the nation's export trade. This prosperity means that Australia enjoys a high standard of living. By mid-2008 full-time earnings had reached $A58,874, with workers in the ACT averaging $68,978 and in Western Australia (where there was a mining boom) averaging $66,404.

THE PEOPLE

Australians are basically gregarious, informal people. Overseas visitors often comment on the willingness of Australians to stop and help a traveller who appears lost, the ready smiles which seem to accompany everyday discourse, and the casual way Australians deal with business activities.

Visitors used to societies which are aggressively driven by customer service will often find that Australian service, particularly in shops, hotels and in the tourist trade, is lax and informal. Australians do not like to see themselves as aggressive. This may come as a surprise to visitors who find that the linguistic tendency to finish a sentence on a rising note sounds abrasive and questioning.

It is important to remember the roots of Australian society. The European community in Australia was almost totally Anglo-Saxon until the 1950s. The resistance to overseas and multicultural impulses was strong. There was, for nearly a century, an informal policy which was dubbed '**the White Australia Policy**' which made entry into the country for non-Anglo-Saxons nearly impossible.

It is also important to recognise that most Australians are proud of the country's convict heritage. Jokes about the society being a collection of descendants of convicts are now totally inaccurate. However, they can be rebutted by proud declarations that Australia is a very egalitarian society (there is only a very small 'upper class' and they are not widely admired) which is based on personal success and whether or not you are a decent and worthwhile human being. Australians dislike people who achieve and

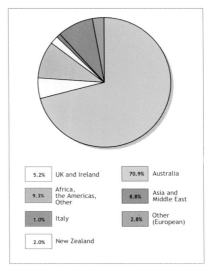

5.2% UK and Ireland	70.9% Australia
9.3% Africa, the Americas, Other	8.8% Asia and Middle East
1.0% Italy	2.8% Other (European)
2.0% New Zealand	

POPULATION CHART BY COUNTRY OF BIRTH

Opposite: *Gum trees reflected in a small creek in South Australia's Flinders Ranges. Red river gums by a creek or river are a natural part of Australia's rural beauty.*

Right: *Multicultural Australia is about drinking cappuccino, eating Thai food, worshipping in a mosque or, like these children in Dutch costume, admiring tulips at a flower farm in Victoria's Dandenong Range.*
Opposite: *One of South Australia's tourist attractions is the Blue Lake at Mount Gambier.*

By June 2008 Australia had 18 urban areas with populations exceeding 100,000. With the exceptions of Canberra and Albury-Wodonga all these urban centres were on the coast. Over 85% of Australians live in urban areas making them one of the most urbanised people on the planet.
The largest cities were:

City	Population
Sydney	4,399,722
Melbourne	3,892,419
Brisbane	1,945,639
Perth	1,602,559
Adelaide	1,172,105
Gold Coast	558,888
Newcastle	531,191
Canberra	345,257
Wollongong	284,169
Sunshine Coast	237,562
Hobart	209,287
Geelong	172,300
Townsville	162,730
Cairns	142,001
Toowoomba	125,339
Darwin	120,652
Launceston	104,649
Albury-Wodonga	102,894

then brashly display their new-found wealth and status. This has been dubbed 'the tall poppy syndrome'. It means that there is a great acceptance of achievement matched with humility and a great intolerance of achievement when it is associated with flashy vulgarity.

Similarly, the country still perceives a deep division between 'workers' and 'bosses'. One theory argues that these feelings date back to convict times when relationships between convicts and overseers were similarly antagonistic.

The Multicultural Mix

After World War II Australia embarked on an active immigration programme. The result of this rapid cultural mix was a huge change in lifestyle. It is hard to imagine that in the early 1950s the average Australian would never have eaten pasta, rarely drunk coffee, probably never bought a bottle of wine and regarded all non-British people as dirty and dangerous.

Today, Australia (particularly the cities) is a truly multicultural society. The average Australian delights in the variety of cuisine available. Thai, Vietnamese, Chinese and Italian restaurants abound, outdoor cafés capitalising on the sunny weather are commonplace, international clothing is popular, and the learning of non-traditional, non-European languages – particularly Japanese and Indonesian – has increased dramatically in schools.

The Aboriginal Society

It is easy when discussing Australian society to ignore the original inhabitants. In recent times Aborigines, who for most of the country's European history had been treated appallingly, have asserted their rights. This hardly redresses the long period of imbalance when they were poisoned, massacred, driven from their land, forced into reserves, treated as social outcasts and had their families torn apart.

Aborigines currently account for 2.5% of the country's population. With a few notable exceptions they live in sub-standard conditions which are characterised by disproportionate levels of unemployment, crime and imprisonment.

The country's Aboriginal and Torres Strait Islander population has been slowly increasing over the past two decades. This may be because more part-Aborigines are registering themselves as Aborigines. It may also be because government programmes are having an effect on lifespan and infant mortality levels. In 1971, there were 115,953 Aborigines registered. This had increased to 458,000 by 2002 and to 517,200 by 30 June 2006. Two-thirds of this population live in Queensland, the Northern Territory and Western Australia.

It has been estimated that the Aboriginal population in 1788 was 300,000–500,000

1860	22,000
1901	93,000
1911	80,000
1921	72,000
1933	81,000
1947	76,000
1961	84,500
1971	116,000
1981	160,000
1991	283,560
1996	353,000
2002	458,000
2006 (est)	517,200

The decline in population is due to introduced diseases, brutality, dispossession and massacres. Its recent increase reflects greater expenditure on welfare and health.

Aboriginal culture is as sophisticated as its technology is simple. Complex ceremonies fusing song, dance, body painting, religion, history and behavioural prescriptions express the lore of the Dreamtime. This embodies the eternal presence, the activities and the unpredictable influence of the beings who were the creators of all things, and the laws relating to interaction with each other and the land. They also tell where to hunt, the location of food and water, and ideal marriage partners.

'**Sacred sites**' are of great significance. They are portions of the landscape which are regarded as incarnations of Dreamtime ancestors.

Opposite: *The beautiful Atherton Tablelands behind Cairns in north Queensland are noted for the dense tropical rainforests and waterfalls. It is said that during the rainy season, when the Millstream Falls near Ravenshoe are in flood, they are the widest falls in Australia.*

In recent years major changes have occurred and the conditions of some Aborigines have improved. Perhaps most significantly in 1994 the federal government converted the high court's '**Mabo**' decision into legislation. This legislation stated that if Aborigines could prove continuous connection with the land they could, under most circumstances, claim that land as their own. This reversed the famous *terra nullius* proposition which was created when Captain Cook stood at Cape York and, in spite of seeing obvious signs of human inhabitation, declared that Australia was uninhabited and, therefore, could legitimately be claimed by the British crown.

Aboriginal Culture

Aboriginal (**Koori**) culture preceded the arrival of Europeans by at least 60,000 years; a period in which it developed in almost complete isolation.

Vital to indigenous culture are the Dreamtime stories concerning the creation and history of the land and its people. Every individual is regarded as a descendant of something in nature, as a part of the spirit which inhabits the land.

Prior to European settlement there were many hundreds of groups with different languages and practices. They lived in relative harmony due to their shared belief in their oneness with the land, which was thought to have been allotted to each tribe in the Dreamtime. The groups traded with each other but maintained and protected their own sacred sites which were taboo to outsiders. There were elders but no chiefs. Laws concerning behaviour were strictly enforced. Men hunted and fished while women collected seeds and roots. Most implements were made of wood. There is evidence of the use of stone tools 10,000 years before they were being used in Europe. Painting, music and dance rituals were integral to everyday life.

When Europeans arrived, the progressive destruction of Aboriginal culture began. Only recently has the problem received attention and some belated understanding.

Australian Culture

Australian cultural life has changed dramatically over the past 50 years. From a narrow cultural world which was based on the proposition that everything from the UK was good and everything that existed in Australia was second-rate, there has been a growing sense of national pride. Today Australians are proud of their multicultural society where differences are accepted.

There is still a tendency to take great pride in overseas recognition. Thus **Patrick White** (who won the Nobel Prize for Literature) and **Thomas Keneally** and **Peter Carey** (who both have won the Booker Prize) are lionised as the country's greatest writers.

Australian films and their makers have also been successful. Jane Campion's *The Piano*, Scott Hicks's *Shine* and Baz Luhrmann's *Strictly Ballroom*, *Romeo and Juliet* and *Australia* have all achieved international recognition and acclaim. Cinematographer Dean Semmler won an Oscar for *Dances with Wolves* and directors Peter Weir, Fred Schepisi and Bruce Beresford have all been nominated. Perhaps Australia's biggest cinematic successes have been Mel Gibson, Russell Crowe, Guy Pearce, Hugh Jackman, Naomi Watts, Cate Blanchett and Nicole Kidman.

The country has a healthy art scene with orchestras of international standing, opera singers starring in the world's great opera houses, ballet dancers and dance troupes receiving international acclaim, and painters and artists (notably the late **Sidney Nolan**) who are represented in the world's great art collections and galleries.

Of course the day-to-day cultural reality for the average Australian is markedly different. The obsessive love of

NATIONAL SYMBOLS

The Australian coat of arms consists of a shield in six parts, each containing a state badge. The ermine border around them represents their federation within a national umbrella. It is supported by two typically Australian animals, the emu and the kangaroo. Behind them is a representative Australian plant, the wattle. The crest, a seven-pointed Commonwealth gold star, is a symbol of national unity.

The Australian national anthem is 'Advance Australia Fair'. The first and last four bars are used in the presence of the governor general while 'God Save the Queen' is still used in the presence of the British Queen. There is an on-going debate about changing the country's flag and national anthem.

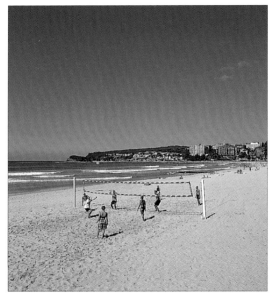

sport, the fascination with television, the unswerving desire to go to pubs, go on picnics, and have a good time outdoors, are still the most vital features of the country's culture. The notion that this is somehow unique to Australia is nonsense. It is just that Australia's working class spreads far into the middle class and thus working-class cultural values – built around sport, recreation and leisure – tend to dominate.

Sport and Recreation

Unlike most countries Australia does not have a large number of national sports. In winter, rugby union and rugby league are played in Queensland and New South Wales; Australian rules in South Australia, Western Australia and Tasmania; and soccer is played throughout the country. The summer sports of cricket, tennis and swimming tend to be nationwide, although the eastern states are more enthusiastic and often win the major competitions such as cricket's state competition.

The strength of Australian sport lies more in the number of people who play it rather than in the number of people who watch it. On any Saturday, in any reasonably sized town or suburb, there will be competitions at the local tennis courts, golf courses, netball courts, and the cricket and football fields. There is also a large amount of purely recreational fishing, bushwalking, swimming (at beaches, local council swimming pools and rivers), and it is very common for outdoor picnics and barbecues to be accompanied by a friendly game of touch football, French cricket or some similarly energetic sport.

Australians are known around the world as a sports-obsessed people. Statistically this can be proven by the following information:
a) 40 per cent of men and 25 per cent of women play some kind of regular sport.
b) In 2007, 615,549 people were regularly playing golf and 362,000 were regularly playing Australian Rules football and soccer has 1,200,000 registered players.
c) In a typical year more than 7 million Australians attend organised sporting events. Australian Rules football attracts the most people, with a total of 2.5 million people attending at least one match in 2005–06.

All this enthusiasm and passion for sport found its finest recent expression in the Sydney 2000 Olympics when Australia successfully hosted the world's most prestigious sporting event. These Olympics attracted 10,651 athletes from 198 countries. Australia came fourth in the medal tally, winning 58 medals including 16 gold medals. Only the US, Russia and China out-performed them.

Food and Drink

There was a time when breakfast consisted of steak, fried tomatoes and eggs. Equally, there was a time when a social lunchtime would ensure that the bar-becue would be lit and sausages, steaks and onions would be cooked. The accompanying tomato sauce, bread, salad and perhaps a rice salad (all washed down with beer for the men and shandies or wine for the women) were part of the fabric of Australian weekend entertainment.

While all of these activities are still common, the con-cern about calorie intake and the increasing variety of foods available as a result of the country's multicultural make-up, have meant that these clichés no longer apply.

It is quite likely that beer at the barbecue has been replaced by a fine wine from the Hunter Valley, the Barossa Valley or the Margaret River area of Western Australia. The sauces may well have given way to something more exotic from Asia, and prawns (shrimp), pieces of fish and chicken are replacing the heavier red meats.

Australians eat and drink well. They are able to do so because they have a high standard of living and because the produce of the country is of a high quality, is readily available and is, by world standards, very cheap.

Overseas visitors quite often gasp in disbelief when they visit a restaurant and find that their bill is less than half what they would pay at home and the food – notable for its freshness – has been better than they could buy in their own country.

One thing that strikes every visitor to Australia is the country's seemingly endless forests of gum trees. They are common in suburban gardens, they grow anywhere the land hasn't been cleared, they are easily ignited and conse-quently are nearly always at the centre of bushfires. They can look grey; on the east coast they can look blue when a fine eucalypt mist rises from them. They are Australia's most distinctive symbol and are a characteristic feature of Australian art.

There are around 700 species of eucalypt, almost all of which occur naturally in Australia. In fact 75% of Australian trees are gums. They range in size and shape from the bush-like mallee and the truncated, gnarled and colourfully streaked snow gums to the jarrah and karri forest giants of Western Australia and the mountain ash of Tasmania and Victoria. They are the tallest flowering plants in the world, attaining heights of 100m (328ft). The fragrant oil of the eucalypt is used in flavourings and pharmaceuticals, the wood often makes excellent timber and its leaves are virtually the sole diet of koalas.

Opposite: *The Australian love of sun, sand and sport finds perfect expression with this social game of volleyball on Sydney's famous Manly beach.*

2
Sydney and New South Wales

State car number plates used to declare 'New South Wales – The Premier State.' In one sense it simply means 'The First State' but in another it means 'The Best State' – the state whose capital city is regarded as one of the most beautiful cities in the world.

The truth is that, while Sydney remains the oldest and largest city in Australia, the state continues to enjoy its 'premier' position. It is, by any definition, a remarkable city. Starting over 200 years ago as a penal colony at the end of the earth, it has dragged itself up by the bootstraps. The beauty of its setting and the mildness of its climate make it a near-perfect place to live.

The beauty of New South Wales extends beyond simply having Sydney as its capital. Although it takes up only 10% of Australia it has a diversity of landform, climate and vegetation which is richer and more complex than any other state, with tropical rainforests in the north, Alpine ski slopes in the south, seemingly endless beaches on the east coast and deserts in the west.

SYDNEY

All explorations of New South Wales, indeed all explorations of Australia, must start with Sydney. It is a city of mild temperatures, of evenly distributed rainfall with slight maximums in the late autumn and early winter, and glorious, balmy, subtropical summer days of sunshine with people sunning themselves on the necklace of beaches which spread to the north and the south of the harbour.

DON'T MISS IN SYDNEY

*** Sydney Opera House: take a tour or just gaze at this remarkable piece of modern architecture.
*** Sydney Harbour Bridge: walk across it or take a tour to the top.
** North Head: offers the best panoramic view of Sydney Harbour.
** Sydney Tower: spectacular views of the city from the city's tallest building.

Opposite: *Designed by Danish architect Jørn Utzon, the Sydney Opera House has become the most recognised symbol of Australia.*

Sydney Area

The cityscape has two monuments: the Sydney Harbour Bridge and the Opera House which mirrors the sails of the yachts racing across the harbour at the weekends.

Sydney started its life as a penal colony. Its first European inhabitants were mostly either soldiers or criminals. Its harbour also became a port where sailors took shore leave, looking for cheap thrills to balance the monotony of life at sea. To appreciate the history of the city, visitors should head towards The Rocks.

City Sightseeing **

A good place to start your exploration of Sydney is **The Rocks.** Although it has now become a series of pubs, restaurants and shops for tourists, it is still possible to see that, in the 18th century, this was the centre of the city's wild military and convict nightlife. When **Circular Quay** was the city's port, the area's solid Victorian sandstone buildings functioned as warehouses. Move east along Circular Quay towards the Opera House and you can catch a ferry across the harbour. The short trip across to **McMahons Point** affords excellent views of the Opera House, passes under the Harbour Bridge, and lands the visitor at the bottom of a hill which leads up to North Sydney, the city's centre of computer technology and advertising.

The Rivercat service to **Parramatta** takes passengers west until the harbour is reduced to a narrow river.

Widely recognised as the two best ferry trips are those to **Taronga Zoo** and to **Manly**. The zoo is beautifully located on the slopes overlooking the harbour, and beyond it is Athol Park which offers delightful walks through bushland. On the trip across to Manly the ferry passes North and South heads and provides many spectacular views of the harbour. On a par with Bondi, Manly is Sydney's second most famous beach. A short walk along The Corso will take the visitor from the harbour-side ferry terminus to the ocean beach.

Beyond Circular Quay is the world-famous **Sydney Opera House**, which has excellent views of the Quay and the Harbour Bridge as well as containing a range of restaurants and coffee shops. The Opera House's numerous theatres range from small drama spaces to concert halls and the main opera theatre itself.

CLIMATE

Sydneysiders feel that they live in a city with a perfect climate. The summers are usually long and sunny. It is, however, common to have summer storms and the city's famous 'southerly buster' – a dramatic cold change often after particularly hot and humid days – is a feature of those hot summer days which sends temperatures tumbling. The winters are mild, and spring and autumn are typically balmy.

Left: *Built between 1923 and 1932, and one of the largest single-span bridges in the world, the Sydney Harbour Bridge is the premier icon of Sydney. Known as 'The Coat-Hanger' or simply 'The Bridge', the main span is 503m (1659ft) long and the top of the arch is 134m (440ft) above sea level.*

TARONGA ZOO

Voted the best international zoo in 1992, Taronga Zoo has superb views of Sydney Harbour and a substantial collection of Australian native fauna. The zoo can be reached by ferry from Wharf 2, Circular Quay (the journey takes 12 minutes) or by bus from Wynyard or St Leonards.
Displays include echidnas, dingoes, wombats, kangaroos and wallabies and Australian snakes and spiders. The koala walkabout and platypus exhibit offer exceptional vantage points of the city. Open 09:00–17:00 every day (http://zoo.nsw.gov.au).

To the east of the Opera House lie the city's **Botanic Gardens** and **Lady Macquarie's Chair**, where the wife of one of the colony's early governors used to sit and enjoy the view across the harbour.

Returning to The Rocks the visitor now heads west. Travelling underneath the Harbour Bridge one passes the old waterfront wharves on the way to **Darling Harbour**.

This is Sydney's equivalent to Fisherman's Wharf in San Francisco. It is a large complex of shops, restaurants and modestly priced eateries, all set against a backdrop of the harbour. Situated at the northern end are the **Sydney Aquarium** and **Sydney Wildlife World**, both showcasing Australian fauna. At the southern end lies the **Chinese Garden of Friendship**, reputedly the largest of its type outside China.

From Darling Harbour the visitor can take the **monorail** into the central business district where department and specialist stores offer a wide range of goods. Most of the major stores have duty-free facilities for tourists.

Eating Out ★★

Just beyond Darling Harbour is Sydney's **Chinatown**. The Chinese settled in Australia during the gold rushes of the 1850s. More recently, large numbers of Asians, many of them refugees from Indo-China, have arrived. Chinatown offers a wide range of Asian cuisine from Vietnam and Thailand, as well as regional varieties of Chinese cooking.

Right: *Sydney is much more than just another modern city of high-rise buildings. Its unique position on one of the world's great natural harbours, and its inviting subtropical parks such as the Botanic Gardens, offer visitors hours of enjoyable scenic walks.*

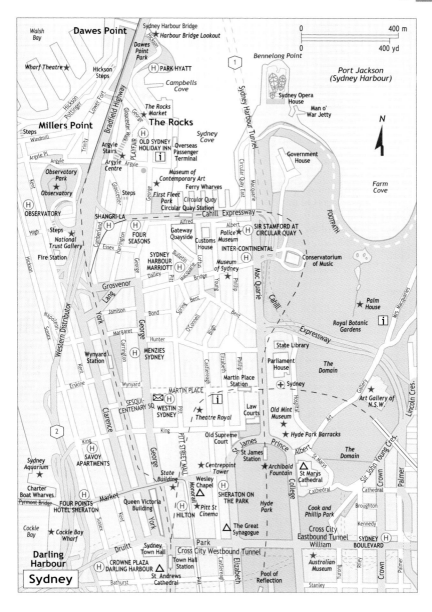

Below: *West of Sydney lie the Blue Mountains, a series of box canyons with sheer cliffs, waterfalls and spectacular views. Travelling on the Katoomba Skyway and looking across at the Three Sisters is both magnificent and hair-raising.*

Museums

Darling Harbour is home to both the **Australian National Maritime Museum** and the **Powerhouse Museum**, a fascinating science and technology museum. On the other side of the city centre is the **Art Gallery of New South Wales**, which offers an excellent overview of Australian art and good collections of international artists. The **Australian Museum** is the nation's oldest and largest natural history museum. Its displays of Australian flora and fauna are considered the finest in the country.

AROUND SYDNEY

There are several interesting daytrips to towns and sights which should be considered part of any visit to Sydney. The most spectacular experience within easy reach of Sydney is that offered by the **Blue Mountains**. On a clear day, from high vantage points near the city, it is easy to see the mountains touched with that distinctive smoky blue which rises from the dense stands of eucalypts.

The mountains were not crossed until 1813. By the 1880s they had become a major tourist attraction and a kind of Australian 'hill station' where people could escape Sydney's summer humidity.

Today, the Blue Mountains have a special charm. The air is bracing – in fact it is quite common for **Katoomba** at 1017m (3337ft) above sea level to have snow in winter. In the 1920s and 1930s it was *the* place for a holiday and hotels such as The Carrington at Katoomba, Cooper's Grand Hotel and the Hydro Majestic at Medlow Bath, gained reputations as places for a *risqué* weekend.

With its spectacular views across the Grose and Jamison valleys, Katoomba is the main tourist attraction. Highlights are the **Three Sisters** on the edge of the Jamison Valley, the

New South Wales

Above: *Quaint, old-fashioned cottages cling to the hillside behind Garie Beach.*

waterfall at **Govett's Leap**, the **scenic railway** at Katoomba, Norman Lindsay's home in Springwood, the **Jenolan Caves** and the **Kanangra Walls**. The views are breathtaking, the eating places are quiet and elegant, and the hotels have a special charm.

Another area beloved of Sydney high society prior to World War II was the **Southern Highlands**. The mildness of the weather, particularly the coolness of the summers, attracted the visitors. The area is home to some of the country's finest cattle studs.

Attractions of the area include the **Wombeyan Caves**, the spectacular **Fitzroy Falls**, the well-preserved historic town of **Berrima**, the gracious gardens of **Bowral** (open in late September during Tulip Festival time) and, especially for cricket lovers, the **Don Bradman Museum** in Bowral. The area is dotted with large homes and hotels.

To the east of the Southern Highlands is the beautiful **South Coast**. The traveller leaving Sydney and heading south first comes to the **Royal National Park** which spreads from the beaches of **Wattamolla** and **Garie** through to the quiet waters of the Hacking River. Covering 14,969ha (37,000 acres) this glorious park lies less than 40km (25 miles) from the centre of Sydney and was Australia's first national park.

Visitors to the park can go surfing, lagoon swimming or fishing. They can have a picnic or spend a day rowing or paddling on the small lake above **Audley Weir**. Or they can walk along the hundreds of bush trails which were developed in the park in the 1920s.

Other areas of particular interest around Sydney are the historic Macquarie towns (**Richmond** and **Windsor**) to the west, the holiday resort area of **Gosford**, and the **Hunter Valley**, the most famed wine-growing area in New South Wales.

THE NEW SOUTH WALES COAST

New South Wales' greatest asset is undoubtedly its 1900km (1180 miles) of coastline. Although the coast has only a few natural harbours, it does have vast numbers of superb beaches.

Along the eastern seaboard lies the fertile coastal plain. It is home to the bulk of the state's dairy industry, vegetable production and tropical fruit plantations. Its agriculture shifts from the bananas, macadamias, pineapples and avocados of the north, to the dairy and beef cattle which are typical of the south coast.

The north coast of New South Wales – **Byron Bay**, **Ballina**, **Yamba**, even as far south as **Port Macquarie** – is an area of tourism, dairy and beef cattle, timber cutting and subtropical plantation farming.

Further south is Newcastle, the state's second-largest city and once a thriving and prosperous steel and coal town. In recent times, with the decline of both its port and its steel industry, Newcastle has successfully transformed itself into an elegant city notable for its excellent restaurants, fine beaches and its proximity to the Hunter Valley, the state's most prosperous wine-growing area.

South of Newcastle, the **Wyong–Gosford** area, once dominated by the cheap weekenders of Sydneysiders, is now a commuter belt. Soaring Sydney land prices and a fast electric train have helped to convert these one-time holiday retreats into Sydney's northernmost suburbs. The Central Coast now reaches beyond Gosford to Toukley and the Tuggerah Lake, Munmorah Lake and Lake Macquarie regions.

To the south of Sydney, the coastal road from **Stanwell Tops** to **Wollongong** is full of surprises. It starts with one of the most spectacular views on the entire east coast of Australia, moves through a series of old coal-mining villages which cling to the edge of cliffs that drop precipitously to the dark waters of the Pacific, and then continues on to New South Wales' third-largest city – Wollongong.

Wollongong is a mixture of industry and tourism. On one level it is a typical steel town. On another level it is edged by a series of excellent beaches. It is possible to lie

ALTERNATIVE LIFESTYLES

The north coast of New South Wales is known as one of the country's most fashionable retreats. Originally dairy farming land it attracted hippies during the 1960s and more recently places like **Byron Bay**, which boast a superb, healthy climate and rural tranquillity, have attracted people eager to escape the pressure of city life including well-known stars including Paul Hogan (of Crocodile Dundee fame), singer Olivia Newton-John and actor Russell Crowe. Today, it is one of Australia's fastest growing holiday destinations.

Above: *Kiama, a delightful seaside holiday-resort town south of Sydney, is famed for its blowhole. When the wind and waves are in the right direction, spumes of spray up to 20m (65ft) high are hurled out of a narrow fissure in the rocks.*

THE SNOWFIELDS

The New South Wales snowfields attract thousands of enthusiastic skiers from all over the world. Each winter the premier resorts of Thredbo village, Smiggin Holes, Perisher Valley, Blue Cow, Crackenback and Charlotte's Pass are filled to capacity with skiers who make the journey from the coast. Artificial snow-making equipment is available if the weather remains too warm. All the resorts have modern chalets and quality ski-lifts.

on the beach without a care in the world while, over the nearest sand dune, gas flames reach high into the sky.

South of Wollongong, the coastal strip is primarily dairy country. It is still common for the traveller driving along a winding country road to be caught behind a herd of Fresians making their way languidly towards the milking sheds. The valleys of the escarpment, with their spectacular array of waterfalls and ferns, lyrebirds, wallabies and wombats, lie close to the coast. However, beyond **Kiama** they fall back making way for the wide floodplain of the Shoalhaven and the white sand beaches which edge **Jervis Bay**.

Jervis Bay is the home of one of the country's major naval training colleges. 7200ha (18 000 acres) of its southern headland was originally handed over to the Commonwealth on the novel grounds that Canberra and the ACT needed a sea port.

Edged by impressive national parks, the far south coast is a series of attractive villages where fishing, timber and dairy industries intermingle.

Eden, on the shores of Twofold Bay, was once a centre for whaling. **Narooma**, **Bermagui**, **Tathra** and **Ulladulla** all have thriving fishing fleets, and towns like **Kameruka**, **Bodalla** and **Bega** are synonymous with the cheeses commonly found on supermarket shelves.

If the north coast is about sun, surf and laziness, the south coast is more rural and more peaceful.

INLAND NEW SOUTH WALES

Beyond the coastal plains of New South Wales lie the magnificent tablelands of the Great Dividing Range. To the south, these tablelands form part of the **Snowy Mountains**, which is the highest mountain range in Australia. It is here that Australia's highest peak, **Mount Kosciuszko**, rises to 2228m (7310ft).

There was a time when the Snowy Mountains were a wilderness of steep ravines, narrow winding dirt roads and white snow gums. It was a superb, untamed region. Then, in 1949, the federal government established the Snowy Mountains Authority and over the next decade a hydro-electricity scheme was developed.

Thousands of workers from all over the world poured into the mountains to work on the vast project. The Snowy Mountains have always been an important subject of a romantic image of Australia. This is the place where the pioneers had to be tough, where the horse riders had to be the best, and where the conditions were most arduous in winter.

Once an area of wilderness and high-country sheep grazing, the mountains are now given over to tourism and electricity production. The old chalets have been replaced by modern, centrally heated hotels and in place of the dirt roads are a ski-tube railway system, high-speed ski-lifts and sealed highways.

For those eager to avoid the crowds, spring and summer are magical times in the mountains. When the skiers go and the snows melt away, the alpine flowers begin to bloom, the kangaroos and wombats reappear and, as the poet 'Banjo' Paterson observed, 'the air is clear as crystal, and the white stars fairly blaze'.

Spring and summer are times for bushwalking, visiting the beautiful **Yarrangobilly Caves**, swimming in the thermal pool, exploring the old gold diggings at **Kiandra**, and climbing to the top of Mount Kosciuszko.

Beyond the Great Dividing Range, New South Wales falls away into a series of low-lying slopes which eventually give way to the plains of the western region.

In turn, as the regular annual rainfall drops below 250mm (10in), these plains dwindle to a scrubby desert which is only good for vast sheep stations where hectares are needed to sustain a single sheep. It is a marginal wasteland where a car can drive along a straight road at 100kph (62mph) for two hours and see nothing other than the occasional kangaroo and endless plains of scrub and bush.

PORTS IN THE DESERT

During the 19th century the Murray and Darling rivers were used extensively by paddle steamers to ship the rich wool clip to the coast. It is hard to imagine that inland towns like Wagga Wagga and Bourke were thriving ports. For decades Bourke was the transport centre for the whole of southwest Queensland and western NSW. At its height in the late 1800s over 40,000 bales of wool were being shipped down the Darling annually. The river transport continued until 1931.

Below: *The snowy slopes at Perisher Valley, Kosciuszko provide a playfield for the young and old.*

Above: *At Lightning Ridge, on the edge of the desert in far northwest New South Wales, miners dig for opals. They are, as one observer noted, 'monuments to the tenacious optimism of all mankind'. The work is hard but the rewards can be great.*

FLORIADE

Canberra is breathtakingly beautiful in both spring and autumn. The decision to plant the city with deciduous European trees and extensive flower beds has meant that the displays of new blooms and changing colours are spectacular. **Floriade**, held every spring (usually October), displays more than half a million flowers and features a fortnight of interesting events.

Towns like **Broken Hill** and **Silverton** have been used as bases for the making of several films such as *A Town Like Alice, Wake in Fright* as well as *Mad Max, Razorback* and a dozen less successful productions. Beyond the film industry, the region is sustained by mining – at Broken Hill, White Cliffs and Silverton – and sheep.

White Cliffs is a town which exists almost entirely underground. The local opal miners, in an attempt to avoid temperatures of over 40°C (104°F) in summer, have dug homes for themselves 10m (33ft) below the surface. There are underground dwellings in White Cliffs which would be considered mansions if they were above the surface. White Cliffs also has a solar energy source to supply the town with electricity.

From **Dubbo**, at the western edge of the central slopes, to **Broken Hill** the traveller drives for hours. The only stopping points on the Mitchell and Barrier highways are isolated townships (a combination of stop-off points for travellers and service centres for the surrounding property owners) such as Nyngan, Bourke, Cunnamulla, and Cobar. These forlorn little settlements put on a brave front to the outside world, but without the highways and the sheep stations they would have no reason to exist.

CANBERRA AND THE AUSTRALIAN CAPITAL TERRITORY (ACT)

Canberra is an artificial city created as a result of the federation of Australian states. In 1908, 2330km² (900 sq miles) of good quality sheep-grazing land was carved out of New South Wales, and on 1 January 1911, the Australian Capital Territory was handed over officially to the commonwealth government.

That same year, a competition was launched for the design of a city for 25,000 people. The competition was won by an American, Walter Burley Griffin, whose design based on a series of geometrically precise circles and axes, was similar to the street patterns of Washington and Paris.

Today, Canberra is a city of great beauty, with broad roadways, superb parklands, and many elegant buildings.

Left: *Canberra's Lake Burley Griffin is a magnet for visitors. There are walks around the lake's edge, boats and bicycles for hire, views across the lake and the spectacular sight of the Captain Cook Memorial Water Jet shooting water up to 140m (460ft) into the air.*

HIGHLIGHTS OF CANBERRA

*** **Parliament House** – excellent art displays and an opportunity to see Australian democracy in action.
*** **Australian War Memorial** – a museum.
** **Old Parliament House** – now a portrait gallery. A fascinating insight into Australian political life.
** **High Court** – a superb modern building. Guided tours are available.
** **Lake Burley Griffin** – walkways and bicycle ways around the lakes shores.
** **National Museum of Australia** – excellent exhibitions on Aborigines, Australian society and history.

On a clear spring or autumn day it is a city which is captivating in its graciousness.

The visitor arriving in Canberra is treated with the kind of attention one would expect from bureaucrats. The information is excellent and it is easy to spend a couple of days visiting the **National Art Gallery** (which now boasts a superb collection of works), the **National Library**, the **Australian War Memorial**, the old and new **Parliament Houses**, the **Film and Sound Archive** (which shows early Australian movies) and the **High Court.**

For people who want simpler pleasures there are boats for hire and a pleasant row or cruise around Lake Burley Griffin offers a very different view of the city.

Sydney and New South Wales at a Glance

BEST TIMES TO VISIT

Sep to **Nov** (spring) Sydney comes alive with parks and gardens full of the city's famous azalea and rhododendron displays. **Dec** to **Feb** (summer) the city, which is abundantly supplied with beaches, certainly knows how to take full advantage of the long, hot summer days.

GETTING THERE

Sydney (Kingsford Smith) **Airport** has both international and domestic terminals. They are 5km (3 miles) away from each other and 9km (6 miles) from the city centre. **Airport Express Buses**, coloured green and gold, operate every 10 minutes from both terminals to well-mapped routes in the city and Kings Cross with stops at most of the major hotels. There is also the **Kingsford Smith Airport Bus** service which operates half hourly and will usually do specified drop-offs and pick-ups; tel: 02 9666 9988. Ring the day before for pick-up service. **Taxis** are plentiful and take you anywhere. Major car rental firms represented at airport. Privately owned shuttle bus companies provide transport between the airport, most Sydney suburbs and regional areas. These buses need to be pre-booked. Check the Yellow Pages under 'Bus and Coach Services' for specific services. Sydney Buses have a service between Bondi Junction and Burwood which includes the T1 International and T3 Domestic Terminals. Clearly marked bus stops are located on the arrivals level of each of these terminals. Information about fares, timetables and connections to other parts of Sydney is available at www.sydneybuses.info Useful websites: www.airportlink.com.au www.sydneybuses.info www, sydneyairport.com.au www.countrylink.info There are railway stations located at the International and Domestic Terminals. The Domestic rail station is located directly between T2 and T3 Terminals and is accessible from within the terminals. The International rail station is located at the northern end of the terminal. Trains run approximately every 10 minutes and the journey into the city takes only 13 minutes. The international and domestic rail stations link directly to the City Circle which means most city destinations are within a short walk of stations.

GETTING AROUND

Sydney has three types of public transport: buses, trains and ferries. All are clearly marked and signposted. For information on these forms of transport ring **Buses, Trains and Ferries**, tel: 13 1500. Timetables for the three services are at the information booth at Circular Quay. The **Explorer**, a tourist bus which operates a continuous loop around the tourist sights, runs every 20 minutes. The stops are marked by green and red signs. Suburban trains are fast and efficient, clearly marked and colour coded. The ferry system is the nicest way to get around. The Taronga Zoo Ferry takes visitors from Circular Quay to the zoo in 12 minutes. Car rental firms are prolific and competitive and are advertised everywhere. Sydney has many hotels, motels and serviced apartments. The central business district has a large range of accommodation, but don't forget the quieter suburban areas. Public transport makes the city centre easy to get to. www.sydneypass.info/sydney explorer

WHERE TO STAY

Westin Sydney Hotel, 1 Martin Place, tel: 02 8223 1111, fax: 02 8223 1222. This centrally located hotel has sympathetically converted the old General Post Office into a luxury experience.
Hotel Inter-Continental, Macquarie St, tel: 02 9253 9000, fax: 02 9240 1240. A luxury hotel partly housed in the historic treasury building (1851) in the centre of the city.
Crown Plaza Darling Harbour, Day St, tel: 02 9261 1188, fax: 02 9261 8766. Opposite the famous Darling Harbour complex, a quality hotel with excellent service.

Sydney and New South Wales at a Glance

Four Seasons Hotel Sydney, George St, tel: 02 9238 0000, fax: 02 9251 2851. The best views in Sydney.

BUDGET ACCOMMODATION
Stafford Apartments, 75 Harrington St, tel: 02 9251 6711, fax: 02 9251 3458. The Rocks, in the heart of the Rocks area, Sydney's oldest district.
Victoria Court Hotel, Victoria St, Potts Point, tel: 02 9357 3200, fax: 02 9357 7606. Breakfast is included in this beautiful old-world boutique hotel, located near both the city centre and Kings Cross.
The Hughenden, 14 Queen St, Woollahra, tel: 1800 64 2432, fax: 02 9362 0398. This 1876 boutique hotel has retained the charm of yester-year with the convenience of a modern hotel.

WHERE TO EAT

Every conceivable variety of food is on offer in this cosmo-politan city. There are several magazines that cover restau-rants comprehensively. *This Week in Sydney* is put out by the NSW Government Tourist Travel Centre. Widely recog-nised as authoritative is the

Sydney Morning Herald's, *Good Food Guide,* available in newsagencies.
Bayswater Brasserie, Kings Cross, tel: 02 9357 2177. Stylish brasserie with excellent service.
Doyles on the Beach, Watsons Bay, tel: 02 9337 2007. Seafood restaurant on the beach overlooking the harbour.
Guillaume at Bennelong, Sydney Opera House, tel: 02 9241 1999. Dine in style at one of Sydney's most famous landmarks.
Golden Harbour Restaurant, 31–33 Dixon St, Haymarket, tel: 02 9212 5987. World-class Chinese restaurant.
Captain Cook Cruises, No. 6 Jetty, Circular Quay, tel: 02 9206 1100. Cruise the harbour and enjoy excellent cuisine.
Jordon's Seafood Restaurant, Darling Harbour, tel: 02 9281 3711. Good seafood served in a fun atmosphere.

TOURS AND EXCURSIONS

Great Sights Daytours, tel: 1300 850 850 or 02 9241 2294. Conveniently located at Circular Quay, this tour com-pany offers a rich diversity of tour options.

Australian Pacific Tours, tel: 02 9247 7222, or 1300 65 5965. Offers a range of coach tours fanning out from Sydney. Their most popular is the daily tour to the Blue Mountains.
Clipper Gray Line, tel: 02 9252 4499 or toll free 1300 858 687. A wide range of coach tours.
Matilda Harbour Cruises, tel: 02 9264 7377. Depart four times a day from Darling Harbour, and the luncheon cruise offers a steak and seafood BBQ.
Captain Cook Cruises, tel: 02 9206 1100. Offers a wonderful look at the Sydney Harbour, ticket is valid all day so you can get off and explore. Departs from Circular Quay.
Heli-Aust Pty Ltd, tel: 02 9791 0322. Enjoy the sites of Sydney from the air.
Tourism New South Wales, 55 Harrington St, tel: 02 9931 1111. Helpful information about what to see and do in NSW is available.

USEFUL CONTACTS

Bridgeclimb, 5 Cumberland St, The Rocks, tel: 02 8274 7777. Climb the Sydney Harbour Bridge for the best view of the famous Sydney Harbour. Advance booking a necessity.
Sydney Visitors Centre, George St, The Rocks, tel: 02 9240 8788, www.sydney visitorcentre.com.au Will answer phone enquiries between 08:00 and 18:00.

SYDNEY	J	F	M	A	M	J	J	A	S	O	N	D
AVERAGE TEMP. °F	73	73	72	66	63	57	54	57	61	64	68	72
AVERAGE TEMP. °C	23	23	22	19	17	14	12	14	16	18	20	22
SEA TEMP. °F	73	75	75	73	70	68	66	63	63	68	68	72
SEA TEMP. °C	23	24	24	23	21	20	19	17	17	20	20	22
RAINFALL in	4	4.5	5	5	5	5	4	3	3	3	3	3
RAINFALL mm	104	117	135	129	121	131	100	81	69	79	82	78
Days of Rainfall	12	12	13	12	12	12	10	10	10	11	11	12

3
Brisbane and Queensland

Queensland is Australia's second-largest state. In spite of its vast size, most of the state is marginal land moving towards desert. If it isn't desert it's impenetrable rainforest or swampy, mangrove wetlands. Consequently, the majority of the state's 4,279,411 (June quarter, 2008) people live in Brisbane or along the coast in large urban sprawls like the **Gold Coast**, the **Sunshine Coast**, and the major cities of **Townsville**, **Bundaberg**, **Cairns** and **Rockhampton**.

The state is cut in half by the Tropic of Capricorn. It is also divided by the Great Dividing Range which starts about 200km (125 miles) south of Cape York, and runs in a series of low-lying ranges and tablelands down the eastern coastline.

Historically, the coast has been one of the state's main agricultural regions. The waters are rich with fish and crustaceans. The slopes of the Great Dividing Range were an important source of valuable tropical timber and the alluvial coastal plains have been ideal for tropical crops such as sugar-cane, pineapples, mangoes, bananas, and pawpaws.

In recent times, agriculture has declined in importance. The great boom industry is tourism. Over 60% of all tourists arriving in Australia nominate Queensland as their primary destination. In 2001, it had over 70 international hotels and tourist resorts, more than a dozen huge marinas, and a network of ancillary facilities such as casinos, charter cruises, sporting complexes, and hundreds of motels and restaurants.

DON'T MISS

*** Botanic Gardens showcasing superb tropical plants beside the Brisbane River.
** Queensland Cultural Centre including the museum and library.
** Moreton Bay and **Stradbroke Island** are well worth a leisurely cruise.
* Government House.

Opposite: *Fraser Island, the largest sand island in the world, is one of the wonders of Queensland. Its quiet, unspoilt beauty symbolises the special charm of much of the Queensland coast.*

Opposite top:
Brisbane is an attractive, modern city where high-rise buildings are mirrored in the quietly flowing waters of the Brisbane River. The city's air of informality makes it different from all the other state capitals.

BRISBANE

In his book, *Portrait of Brisbane*, Bill Scott wrote: 'Brisbane is a lazy town with its sleeves rolled up, casually sprawling across its thirty-seven hills.'

This image of a subtropical city which thrives on informality still captures the spirit of the city today.

Brisbane is no ordinary state capital. Queensland, because of its size and its decentralisation, can claim Brisbane as its centre of government while still acknowledging the regional importance of cities like **Townsville** and **Rockhampton.**

City Sightseeing

Brisbane has long had a tradition of newness and, as a result, it has relatively few genuinely old public buildings of importance. However, the remaining old buildings are gracious and impressive.

The most interesting landmarks in the city include **The Old Windmill**, sometimes known as **Observatory Tower**, and the **The Old Commissariat Store** at 111 William Street which was built by convicts when Brisbane was a closed penal colony. It is now the head-quarters of the Royal Historical Society of Queensland.

Another significant landmark is the **City Hall Art Gallery** and **Museum** complex, which combines **King George Square**, the **Brisbane Administration Centre** and the **City Plaza Shopping Centre**. The clock tower, which rises 91m (300ft) above the City Plaza, provides excellent panoramic views of the city.

CLIMATE

Brisbane's climate is sub-tropical with an average annual rainfall of 1090mm (43in), most of which falls between December and March, an average of over seven hours of sunshine each day, a humidity level which hovers around 50% for all the year, and a temperature range from 10°C (50°F) in winter to 30°C (86°F) in summer.

CITY OF TROPICAL PARKS

Brisbane's warm, moist climate ensures that the city's 200 parks and gardens are its greatest attraction. Be sure to see the dome-shaped indoor display at Mount Coot-tha which houses a virtual tropical rainforest and the displays of orchids, flame trees, bougainvilleas, frangipanis, oleanders and jacarandas, which make the City Botanic Gardens so impressive. The park at South Bank offers excellent views of the city.

Left: *Brisbane's South Bank complex offers a cultural centre, a performing arts centre and a swimming pool, which is more in keeping with a faraway tropical island than the centre of a modern city.*

MOUNT COOT-THA BOTANIC GARDENS AND RESERVE

Located off Mount Coot-tha Road in Toowong, only 10 minutes from the city centre, the Mount Coot-tha Gardens are reputed to be Australia's largest subtropical display of flora. They cover an area of 57ha (140 acres) in which plants are set against an environment of lakes, ponds and streams. The indoor displays ensure that even in winter the gardens are worth a visit.

Located just over the Victoria Bridge from the city's central business district is **South Bank**. This includes the **John Oxley Library**, the **Queensland Museum** with its two million items, including the tiny 'Avian Cirrus' aeroplane in which Bert Hinkler made the first solo flight from England to Australia in 1928, and the **Performing Arts Complex** with its Lyric Theatre, Concert Hall and Cremorne Studio Theatre.

At 261 Queen Street, the **General Post Office** is located on the site of the city's original female convict barracks. On the first floor is the GPO Museum which exhibits a range of old postal, radio and telegraphic equipment.

Located between the **Queensland Institute of Technology** and the **Brisbane River** is the **old Government House,** which was built in 1862. It is currently used as the offices for the National Trust of Queensland.

The **Queensland Maritime Museum** is situated on the river at the end of Dock Street. The museum features an interesting display of charts, model ships, engines and memorabilia, combined with 'on the water' displays of a World War II frigate and an old steam tug.

In Petrie Terrace, the old **Victoria Barracks** were built between 1864 and 1874 to a design which had been drawn up by the War Office in London. Today, the barracks are a military museum housing weapons, old uniforms, photographs and memorabilia.

Parks and Gardens

Brisbane has nearly 200 parks and reserves within the city. The City Botanic Gardens cover over 20ha (50 acres) of land. Beautifully located on the banks of the Brisbane River and spreading over the gentle slopes and undulations below Parliament House and the old Government House, the gardens are a peaceful respite from the bustle of the central business district.

THE GOLD COAST

The Gold Coast is Australia's most famous tourist area. Since the 1950s, it has developed to house innumerable motels and hotels, eateries, a casino and several high-profile attractions: **Warner Bros. Movie World**, **Wet 'n' Wild** and **Sea World.**

The high-rise development which has occurred along the coast has not met with universal approval. Still, the area continues to act as a magnet. Its population doubles every decade. It attracts thousands of holiday-makers during the summer months, and its New Year's Eve Party and end-of-school celebrations have become legendary.

In the hinterland behind the Gold Coast there are stretches of unspoilt rainforest, spectacular waterfalls and the beautifully rugged Lamington National Park. The peacefulness of the villages and the quietness of the shops stands in sharp contrast to the exuberance of the coast.

GOLD COAST BEACHES

There are nine major beaches along the Gold Coast. Each is excellent for sunbathing, swimming and surfing.
● Coolangatta – fun for the whole family.
● Currumbin – more famous for its bird sanctuary than its beach.
● Palm Beach.
● Burleigh Heads.
● Nobby Beach.
● Mermaid Beach.
● Broadbeach – in the heart of the tourist action.
● Surfers Paradise – the most famous of all the beaches. A long sandy strip backed by high-rise apartments.
● Southport – the more modern and exclusive end of the coast.

GOLD COAST HOLIDAY ATTRACTIONS

There's the multimillion dollar **Conrad International Hotel** complex which includes **Jupiters Casino** where popular Japanese gambling games like Keno and Sic-Bo vie with Baccarat, Roulette, Blackjack and the all-Australian Two-up. There's **Sanctuary Cove** and the low-rise luxury of the **Sheraton Mirage Gold Coast** with its marina and lagoon. The **Wet'n'Wild Water World** has the only man-made pool in Australia with one-metre waves and lifeguards, and the exclusive Sanctuary Cove boasts an 18-hole golf course designed by Arnold Palmer.

Opposite: *The Great Barrier Reef is one of the wonders of the world. There is no better way to experience its beauty than to sail to the outer reef and explore the wonderland of fish and coral formations.*
Right: *First sighted and named by Captain Cook, the Glasshouse Mountains north of Brisbane, are a series of volcanic plugs (the surrounding material has been slowly eroded away) of rhyolite and trachyte, estimated to be between 24 and 25 million years old.*

THE SUNSHINE COAST

Travelling north from Brisbane, the visitor must first pass through the **Sunshine Coast** to beautiful **Fraser Island** (the largest sand island in the world), through the beef and cattle country between **Gladstone** and **Mackay**, and the densely covered tropical rainforest areas which stretch from **Townsville** to **Cape York**.

Nothing captures the spirit of the Sunshine Coast quite like the **Big Pineapple**, a theme park based on pineapple production. To indicate its entrance, a huge replica of a pineapple sits, golden and gleaming, beside the Bruce Highway, just south of **Nambour**. 'Take a genuine Sugar Cane Train ride, hop aboard the fun Nutmobile. Little ones will love petting the kangaroos,' declares the advertisement.

Lying north of Brisbane, the Sunshine Coast has developed rapidly as a major attraction for tourists. Its advantages are largely connected to a more up-market appeal. A thriving centre like **Noosa**, now the home of tennis champion Evonne Cawley, is far more sophisticated than any part of the Gold Coast.

Historically, this was a typical tropical rural area. In recent times, the agricultural base has expanded to include ginger, macadamia nuts and lesser-known tropical fruits.

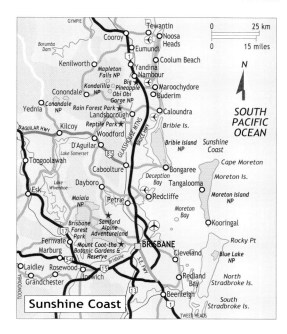

Sunshine Coast

Away from the coast, in the area around the spectacular extinct volcanoes of the **Glasshouse Mountains**, for example, dairy farming is still the dominant industry.

The area has become a popular tourist destination for people from both Melbourne and Sydney. it is dotted with charming haute cuisine restaurants and there are many five-star hotels.

THE GREAT BARRIER REEF ★★★

The Great Barrier Reef is made up of more than 2100 separate reefs and covers over 230,000km² (88,780 sq miles). It is the largest structure built by living creatures.

The cliché 'underwater wonderland' is a remarkably apt description of the Reef. Its formations, from the huge red sea fans to the luxuriant coral cays, are breathtaking and its fish, crustaceans, anemones and sea wasps (more commonly known as box jellyfish) are mysterious, beautiful and exotic.

FRASER ISLAND

Fraser Island ranks as one of the true wonders of Australia. It is the largest sand island in the world and has such a range of attractions and activities that it is a 'must' for anyone travelling along the Queensland coast. It is on Fraser Island that the visitor can see extraordinary freshwater sand dune lakes, beautiful quiet streams, cliffs with remarkable coloured sand horizons, and rugged headlands.

TJAPUKAI ABORIGINAL CULTURAL PARK

Located next to the Skyrail Rainforest Cableway, the Tjapukai Aboriginal Cultural Park comprises three theatres, a museum, an art gallery and a traditional Aboriginal camp. It is an extraordinary cultural experience which leaves the visitor with a profound under-standing of the richness of Aboriginal culture and the difficulties Aborigines have experienced since the arrival of Europeans on Australian shores. The highlight is the Tjapukai Dance Theatre where dancers and singers present a show which is a powerful mixture of ancient and modern designed to help the visitor to understand aspects of Aboriginal life. The show is infused with a buoyant sense of humour and there is a constantly reiterated theme of 'Proud to be an Aborigine'.

The economy of the Reef is based on tourism. There are 25 island resorts, including the coral cays of Heron, Green and Lady Elliot islands and the resorts of Magnetic Island near Townsville, Dunk Island and the Whitsunday group (which includes South Molle, Daydream, Brampton, Lindeman, Hayman and Hamilton islands).

From the mainland the most popular centres for exploring the Reef are at Townsville and Cairns.

CAIRNS

Cairns is a boom town. Tourism has seen it change from a quiet port to an international destination. It is an ideal access point to the Great Barrier Reef and the skyrail-train journey from Cairns to Kuranda offers the visitor a unique opportunity to experience tropical rain-forest from a gondola and a small train.

The **Tjapukai Aboriginal Cultural Park**, which is situated next to the Skyrail Rainforest Cableway, is a superb introduction to Aboriginal life and culture, and well worth a visit.

THE FAR NORTH

To the west and north of Cairns lies the Far North of Queensland – a region characterised by tropical rainforest along the coast, dry inland areas, and one of the richest concentrations of flora and fauna anywhere in Australia. This is an area of vast distances, few towns – **Mossman**, **Port Douglas**, **Weipa**, **Cooktown** – and a few tiny settlements like **Bamaga** at the tip of the **Cape York Peninsula**. The rough dirt roads are often cut by creeks and rivers.

The road from Cairns to Bamaga is over 900km (560 miles) long. The local Aborigines live on outlying reserves and the only industry of any importance began in 1955, when Weipa was confirmed as the site of the largest bauxite deposit in the world.

Because of the poor roads and inhospitable terrain, much of Cape York has remained untouched, but there are some wonderful national parks that are worth the hike. Only the area between Cairns and Cooktown has been subject to any kind of commercial and agricultural development. In this area, tropical fruit is grown, tea plantations have been established, and both commercial and game fishing are practised.

There has been controversy about the development of the **Daintree** for tourism, but it is a marvellous experience to cross the Daintree and move through the tropical rainforest to Cape Tribulation with its mangrove coastline.

Opposite: The Aboriginal dancers in the Tjapukai Aboriginal Cultural Park are dedicated to the preservation and portrayal of Aboriginal dance.

Around Cairns

Right: *Port Douglas, north of Cairns, is one of Queensland's most luxurious resort towns. Once a wild gold-mining port, it is now noted for its chic shopping facilities and Barrier Reef cruises.*
Opposite: *The marker a few kilometres from the Combo Waterhole reminds visitors of its link to Australian history.*

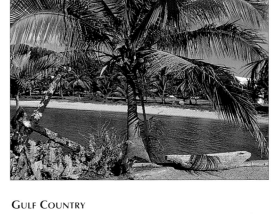

GULF COUNTRY

The Gulf Country is bounded by the Great Dividing Range and the Atherton Tablelands to the east, the Northern Territory to the west, and the Gulf of Carpentaria to the north.

This is a wilderness of mangrove swamps with a summer monsoon season when temperatures climb over 40°C (over 104°F), the humidity is unbearable and the heavy monsoonal rains fall with monotonous regularity.

But the Gulf is more than a dangerous wilderness. **Karumba**, the sole port of the Gulf, is home to both a prawning fleet and Queensland's lucrative barramundi industry. Croydon was once the centre of an important gold-mining industry and gems like topaz, garnet and aquamarine can still be found in the eastern savannah.

The real interest of the Gulf lies in the antiquity of its Aboriginal culture (it is known that Aborigines have lived there continuously for the last 35,000 years) and the extraordinary richness of its wildlife.

BEYOND THE COAST

Queensland is a vast flat area which slowly moves from savannah grassland to desert beyond the coast. The towns are isolated, the accommodation is basic and often the water supply comes from artesian bores, bubbling up from hundreds of metres below the surface.

The whole area is marginal agricultural land and it ceases to be even marginal when the edge of the **Simpson Desert National Park** is reached some 100km (62 miles) to the west of Birdsville. Life here can be hard and the people justifiably regard their lonely existence with considerable pride.

Throughout the inland there are places which mean a lot to Australians. The **Combo Waterhole** near **Kynuna** is said to be the billabong into which 'Banjo' Paterson's jolly swagman jumped. The tiny hotel at **McKinley** was renamed 'Walkabout Creek' for Paul Hogan's *Crocodile Dundee*. **Mount Isa** is the world's largest single producer of lead and zinc and the largest city in the world (in area) covering a total of 41,255km² (16,000 sq miles).

The inland is also noted for its rich diversity of wildlife. Brolgas, flocks of black and white cockatoos, wild pigs, corellas, kangaroos and emus abound. If the rains of the monsoonal wet season reach the headwaters of the dusty **Diamantina** and **Cooper Creek** rivers, large areas of the southwest can be converted into a vast lake.

This is still frontier land. It is harsh and inhospitable with roads suitable for four-wheel-drive vehicles only.

STOCKMAN'S HALL OF FAME

The A$12.5-million 'Australian Stockman's Hall of Fame' at Longreach is the premier destination in central Queensland. It should be called 'The Australian History Timeline'. Its exhibitions include a model of Aboriginal cave paintings, the First Fleet, the early settlement in Sydney, the major explorations, the early pioneers (with a model slab hut, a hawker's van and a blacksmith's shop), the pastoral expansion, and then a focus on life in the bush up to the present day.

Brisbane and Queensland at a Glance

Queensland's seasons are divided into a 'wet' and a 'dry'. During the 'wet', rain and cyclones hit the coast. This occurs through the summer months. The best time to visit is from **Jun** to **Sep** (dry). This is officially winter, however, the days are warm and balmy and the nights cool and pleasant.

The Brisbane **international** and **domestic airports** are close to each other and are about 12km (8 miles) northeast of the city centre. **Coachtrans** runs a shuttle bus from both terminals to the Transit Centre in the city every half hour from 05:00–23:00. Brisbane's Airtrain is the fastest and cheapest way to get to central Brisbane from the airport. There is also a direct service to the Gold Coast. www.airtrain.com.au **Taxis** are available at both airports as are the major **car rental** firms. The **Transit Centre** in Roma St is the main terminus and booking point for all long-distance trains and buses. Brisbane is well serviced by both. The XPT train from Sydney takes 14 hours and runs daily. The major bus companies all travel to and from the capital cities to Brisbane.

Brisbane's bus service is efficient and easy to use. Bus-stops are colour-coded for convenience. The **city circle** bus does a clockwise loop every five minutes. The **Citytrain** network has seven lines running to the suburbs. All trains go through the Transit Centre in Roma St. Car rental firms are well represented. All the major companies operate and there are also many smaller rental agencies. The **Brisbane River** is an active waterway, particularly for visitors. It flows through the centre of the city. There are a number of ferry and cruise ships offering interesting journeys along the river.

Brisbane is both a tourist destination and the capital of Queensland. As such it has a thriving city centre and a wide range of accommodation, offering everything from luxury five-star serviced apartments to bed and breakfast.
Stamford Plaza Brisbane, cnr Margaret & Edwards sts, tel: 07 3221 1999, fax: 07 3221 6895. Centrally located, luxurious hotel near waterside and Botanic Gardens.
Brisbane Marriott Hotel, 515 Queen St, tel: 07 3303 8000, Fax: 07 3303 8088. Overlooking the Brisbane River, this five star hotel offers elegance and sophistication.
Quay West Suites Brisbane, 132 Alice St, tel: 07 3853 6000, fax: 07 3853 6060. Every modern luxury is included in this 5 star hotel. Close to City Botanic Gardens.

BUDGET ACCOMMODATION
Chifley on George, George St, tel: 07 3221 6044, fax: 07 3221 7474. Centrally located, well-priced hotel, with all the facilities of a more expensive hotel.
Holiday Inn Brisbane, Roma St, tel: 07 3238 2222, fax: 07 3238 2288. Good clean accommodation with excellent facilities; well located.
Mercure Hotel Brisbane, North Quay, tel: 07 3237 2300, fax: 07 3236 1035. Overlooks the Brisbane River and South Bank parklands, central location.
Metro Inn Tower Mill, 239 Wickham Terrace tel: 07 3832 1421, fax: 07 3835 1013. Comfortable rooms at a reasonable price.

Brisbane has a large and varied selection of restaurants catering for all tastes. Queensland is famous for its seafood: mud crab, Moreton Bay bugs and barramundi. Check *This Week in Brisbane* and also *Dining Out*.
Breakfast Creek Wharf Restaurant, 192 Breakfast Creek Rd, Newstead, tel: 07 3252 2451, fax: 07 3252 2655. Exceptional seafood.
Augustine's on George, 40 George St, tel: 07 3221 9365. Quality restaurant, centrally located.
Vino's Restaurant & Bar, upper level Eagle Street Pier, tel: 07 3221 0811.

Brisbane and Queensland at a Glance

Overlooking the Brisbane River, Vino's has a modern Australian menu, with a European influence. It also boasts a well stocked bar.
Mount Coot-tha Summit Restaurant, Mount Coot-tha, tel: 07 3369 9922. An incredible view over the city and out to Moreton Bay at this mountain-top restaurant.
Pier Nine, cnr Mary & Eagle sts, tel: 07 3226 2100. Fresh fish cooked with flair; lovely river views.
Siggi's at the Post Office, cnr Edward & Margaret sts, tel: 07 3221 1999. Part of the Stamford Plaza Hotel, elegant award-winning restaurant; fine dining.

Tours and Excursions

Brisbane Paddlewheeler, tel: 07 3630 2666. Departs from Pier 1, Queens Wharf Rd. This old-world paddlewheeler cruises the Brisbane River both day and night.
Scenic Hinterland Holiday Day Tours, tel: 07 5531 5536, www.hinterlandtours.com.au Offer a wide variety of tours including both coastal and hinterland journeys.
Captain Cook Cruises, tel: 1800 804 843 (toll free). Three-, four- and seven-day cruises to the Great Barrier Reef from Cairns which include reef-diving, visiting coral atolls and exploring islands on the reef.
Traveltrain Services, Transit Centre, Roma St, tel: 07 3235

3291. An inexpensive and enjoyable way to discover Brisbane.
Mirimar Cruises, Queens Wharf Rd, North Quay, tel: 1300 729 742. Daily trips to Koala Sanctuary.
Just Cruiz'n Cruises, tel: 07 3880 1971, info@justcruizn cruises.com.au Discover Moreton Bay and enjoy an on-board lunch with the friendly staff.

Queensland Adventure Safaris, tel: 07 5502 4000. Tours of the Daintree Rainforest, Cape Tribulation and Kuranda occur daily leaving from Cairns and Port Douglas.
A large number of tour operators can be booked through the Queensland Government Travel Centre.
Save the Koala Tours, tel: 07 3229 7233, run a tour to the Lone Pine Koala Sanctuary. This is Australia's best known animal sanctuary.
AB Sea Cruises, tel: 07 3893 1240. Visit historic St Helena Island, an early penal colony; also offer charter trips.

Fly Me To The Moon, tel: 07 3423 0400, fax: 07 3423 0500. Early morning hot-air ballooning over Brisbane city, Beenleigh and Gatton. A wonderful way to see the beauty of Queensland. Champagne breakfast on landing.

Useful Contacts

Royal Automobile Club of Queensland, Queen St, tel: 1800 629 501, www.racq.com.au Offers a comprehensive series of road maps and helpful Information.
Queensland Environmental Protection Agency, tel: 07 3227 8185, www.epa.qld.gov.au Great for explorers and bush walkers located on Ann St, open Mon–Fri during business hours.
Holiday Services Tours and Cruises, tel: 07 3236 1054. Conveniently located at the Transit Centre, can provide information on Brisbane and the surrounding areas.
Brisbane Visitor Information Centre, Queen St Mall, tel: 07 3229 5918, www. brisbanetourism.com.au

BRISBANE	J	F	M	A	M	J	J	A	S	O	N	D
AVERAGE TEMP. °F	77	77	75	72	66	63	61	64	68	72	75	77
AVERAGE TEMP. °C	25	25	24	22	19	17	16	18	20	22	24	25
SEA TEMP. °F	77	77	77	77	73	72	68	66	66	66	72	73
SEA TEMP. °C	25	25	25	25	23	22	20	19	19	19	22	23
RAINFALL in	6	6	5	4	3	2.5	2	2	2	3	4	5
RAINFALL mm	160	158	141	94	74	68	57	47	46	76	97	134
Days of Rainfall	13	13	15	11	10	8	7	7	7	5	10	12

4
Melbourne and Victoria

Covering 227,620km² (87,900 sq miles), only 3% of mainland Australia, Victoria is the smallest of all the mainland states.

Melbourne has been, for significant periods in Australia's history, the country's unofficial capital city. In 1888, the year of the country's centennial celebrations, Melbourne was the most populous city in Australia, and it was the seat of Federal Government until the Parliament House was built in Canberra.

Victoria, or the Port Phillip District as it was known, remained part of New South Wales until 1851. It was settled in 1803 by **Lieutenant David Collins** who, with a small group of convicts and free settlers, established a camp at Port Phillip Bay.

Collins was followed by **John Batman**, who, in June 1835, signed a treaty with the local Aborigines and 'purchased' 243,000ha (600,000 acres) from them.

Today, Victoria is a state rich in resources, with a strong and productive economic base. Despite its size it is home to over 25% of Australia's population.

Primarily a fine wool and fat lamb producer, it is also a beef, wheat and dairy producer, with nearly three million beef cattle and 1.5 million dairy cattle in the state.

MELBOURNE

Melbourne is the capital of Victoria. It is a sophisticated and cultured modern city and is now recognised as the second-largest city in Australia with a population of 3.9 million in 2009.

DON'T MISS

*** National Gallery of Victoria: one of the finest in Australia with excellent exhibitions and permanent displays of works by Australia's best artists.
** The Yarra River: may be muddy but walks along the banks and cruises are well worth the stroll.
** Captain Cook's Cottage: in the Fitzroy Gardens, was brought out to Australia from England.
** Tram: travelling around the inner city is a must.

Opposite: *The parks along both sides of the Yarra River are ideal for walking, picnics and barbeques.*

CLIMATE

Melbourne has a mean average temperature of 15°C (59°F) and an annual rainfall of 657mm (26in) which rises to 889mm (35in) in the ranges to the west of the city.

The city has a reputation for unreliable weather. Even locals will admit that the weather can provide four seasons in one day.

It is a city suffering from urban sprawl. Ribbons of urban development spread out into the commuter belts of the Dandenong Range and the beachside suburbs.

Gold gave the city its greatest boost. It saw the establishment of roads, railway lines and a substantial water reservoir. As the population of the city grew, so the demands upon the surrounding agricultural lands became tailored to the needs of the local community. Dairy farms provided the city with milk. Crops of domestic vegetables were grown on the plains, while orchards were planted in the nearby mountains.

It is very easy for first-time visitors to find their way around the centre of Melbourne. The city is set out in a simple grid pattern.

Below: *With the gold rushes of the 1850s, Melbourne became the cultural and financial centre of Australia. Today, its modern high-rise buildings are a reminder that this city beside the Yarra is still a vital commercial centre.*

City Sightseeing

The central business district is unique in the way it blends the Victorian architecture of the city's boom period with modern high-rise buildings. This is not an accidental design decision. As long ago as 1971, committees were formed to plan Melbourne's development to the year 2000. Part of this plan was to strike a balance between modern development and a sense of history.

A sensible starting point is **West Gate Bridge**, which rises 54m (177ft) above the Yarra River, and offers a fine panorama of the city, as does the view from the Rialto Towers Observation Deck in Collins Street.

Other ways of seeing the city include hot-air ballooning, canoeing at Albert Park Lake and taking a cruise across Port Phillip Bay.

The city centre is notable for its wide range of historic buildings. The **Block Arcade**, which dates from 1892, is a fine example of a Victorian shopping arcade. The **Rialto Building**, at 497 Collins Street, is a marvellous Italian Gothic building symbolic of the affluence of the 1890s, and the **Royal Arcade** (1869), at 331 Bourke Street, is a reminder of the wealth that flowed into the city after the gold rushes at Bendigo and Ballarat.

Shopping

Melbourne is regarded, certainly by Victorians, as the best shopping centre in Australia. **Bourke Street**, **Collins Street**, the Block Arcade off Collins Street and the Royal Arcade off Bourke Street are noted for their elegant, expensive boutiques.

Beyond the city centre are **Toorak Road** (the road of the city's elite, with a selection of expensive boutiques and clothing shops), and **Chapel Street** with its attractive, specialist boutiques.

Things to Do

No visit to Melbourne is complete without experiencing the **Yarra River**. It is possible to enjoy picnics on the banks. It is also possible to hire canoes, to sit in restaurants which are moored along the banks, to go cycling along the **Yarra River Cycle Track** or to join a variety of cruises, many of which serve delicious food and wine.

Melbourne is home to **Australian Rules Football**. Visitors during the football season should not miss out on this unique and fast-moving game. It is a strange combination of rugby, soccer and Gaelic football and has almost become the state's religion.

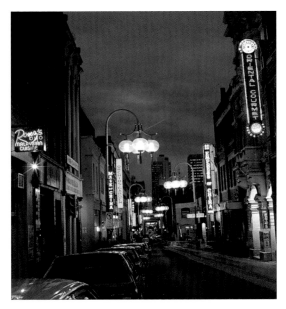

People interested in the history of Melbourne can join any number of organised **Heritage Walks** around the city or purchase Heritage Walk brochures and explore historic sites at their own pace.

Melbourne is now the only major Australian city which still operates a wide-ranging **tram service**. This delightful form of transportation is an integral part of city life. It is possible to buy a day ticket and to use the trams to explore the city's central business district as well as the suburbs.

Eating

Melbourne is noted for the diversity and quality of its cuisine. The city boasts excellent Asian restaurants, superb French nouvelle cuisine and European ethnic eateries. Still, there is nothing to compare with the concentration of Italian restaurants on **Lygon Street**. The *Age Good Food Guide* is an annual publication which lists restaurants according to the style of cuisine.

Parks, Gardens, Museums and Galleries

The city has excellent parks, notably the **Royal Botanic Gardens** and the **King's Domain Gardens**, with **La Trobe Cottage** (1839) and the **Shrine of Remembrance**, and **Fitzroy Gardens** with **Captain Cook's Cottage** which was transported from its original location in Yorkshire.

The **Arts Centre of Victoria** includes the superb **National Gallery of Victoria** which has one of the country's best collections of Australian art. The front façade with its water walls is breathtaking.

AROUND VICTORIA

Although it is a small state, Victoria is diverse and unusual. It offers both the snowfields of the **Snowy Mountains** and the deserts of the **Wimmera** and **Mallee**; and the spectacular formations which draw people to the **Great Ocean Road** as well as the old gold-mining towns of **Stawell**, **Bendigo** and **Ballarat**.

The Central Highlands

Lying to the northwest of Melbourne is Victoria's Central Highlands. The region was settled in the 1830s by about 70 squatters who turned the land into one of Australia's most productive fat lamb and wool areas.

In 1851, gold was found at the tiny settlement of Clunes. In the next year, gold was discovered at over 20 sites in the highlands and gold fever brought tens of thousands of new settlers to the area. Once the initial excitement and the possibility of picking nuggets of gold from the ground began to wane, the area returned to agriculture.

PUBLIC GARDENS

● **Royal Botanic Gardens** – features flowerbeds, trees, lawns and lakes. Open daily 07:30–20:30 Nov–Mar; 07:30–18:00 Apr, Sep and Oct; 07:30–17:30 May–Aug. The **National Herbarium** has a large collection of dried plants including some of those gathered by Joseph Banks during Captain Cook's voyage to Australia in 1770.

● **King's Domain Gardens** include La Trobe Cottage. This cottage was brought to Australia in 1839 to house the city's first governor, Charles Joseph La Trobe. It is currently open only for booked tour groups.

● **Treasury Gardens** – grassy lawns and old shady trees. There is a memorial to John F Kennedy beside the lake.

● **Flagstaff Gardens** – a beautiful terraced garden overlooking Port Phillip Bay.

Opposite: *Melbourne's substantial Chinese community is one of the legacies of the gold-rush era. Today, Chinatown in Little Bourke Street offers the visitor a wide range of Chinese and Southeast Asian cuisine.*

Melbourne Area

Although **Ballarat** and **Bendigo** both have an important industrial sector the biggest growth industry is tourism. The jewel of the area's tourism is found at **Sovereign Hill**, where an 1850s gold-mining town has been convincingly recreated.

Ballarat has a Gold Museum, a memorial to the **Eureka Stockade** and a **Fine Art Gallery** with an exceptional collection of Australian paintings.

SOVEREIGN HILL

Sovereign Hill's main street evokes a mining town's ambience. There is also a Government Camp with an officers' quarters, a court-house and military barracks. It is easy to spend a day at this impressive recreation of a 19th-century gold-mining town. You can pan for gold (and actually get small nuggets), inspect the various shops, watch the blacksmith at work and, at night, watch the spectacular 'Blood on the Southern Cross', a recreation of the Eureka Stockade riot.

Right: Bendigo is one of Victoria's great 19th-century gold-mining towns. At the centre of the town are the beautiful Conservatory Gardens.

Left: *Sovereign Hill is a total recreation of a 19th-century gold-mining town with shops, pubs, mining facilities and even a horse-drawn stagecoach.*

Gippsland

To the east of Melbourne lies Gippsland, encompassing an area which stretches from **Western Port** around **Wilsons Promontory** and north along the coast to the New South Wales border.

The Great Dividing Range is a real challenge. This seemingly inhospitable, heavily forested area is sparsely populated even today. It falls away sharply to the plains which stretch across to **Ninety Mile Beach** and encompass the lakes which lie between Bairnsdale and Sale.

In the 1860s, with the major goldfields in the Central Highlands nearly exhausted, Government surveyors moved into the Gippsland area hoping to find fields which would keep the itinerant miners in Victoria.

The area was never a truly successful gold-mining region. About as close as gold fever ever came was the town of Walhalla, where gold was discovered in 1862.

Access to Melbourne as a result of the construction of a railway line saw the rapid expansion of dairying in the area and by the 1930s, Gippsland had become Melbourne's major supplier of dairy produce.

The real economic wealth of the state of Victoria lies in its coal deposits. Since 1824, it had been known that coal existed in Gippsland.

BENDIGO

Bendigo's gold-rush days have left it with an unusual range of attractions including a **Chinese joss house**, a number of **wineries** and the **Central Deborah Mine** which was mined for over a century, yielding 690 million grams (over 240 million ounces) of gold. Bendigo Heritage Tours conduct tours of Central Deborah Goldmine and they also operate the 'Talking Trams' which run from the terminus at the Central Deborah Goldmine through the heart of Bendigo to the Chinese joss house, also stopping at the Tram Museum. For details contact tel: 03 5443 8255.

GIPPSLAND

Victoria has traditionally had a strong industrial base. Gippsland, for example, is the centre of Victoria's coal and power industries, and cities like Morwell provide the state with locally manufactured coal briquettes and electricity from the Yallourn Power Station. An added economic impetus occurred in the 1960s, when the Esso–BHP consortium discovered oil and gas off the coast.

Above: *The Snowy Mountains, Australia's favourite ski destination, are only a few hours north of Melbourne. In winter Victorians travel to popular resorts such as Mt Buller to enjoy the snow.*

NORTHEASTERN VICTORIA

From Swan Hill on the Murray River across to the Snowy Mountains and their numerous ski resorts, the northeastern region of Victoria is characterised by great diversity. To the east the region is mountainous and experiences snow and sub-zero temperatures during winter. The mountains fall away to gently undulating slopes and by Swan Hill it is monotonously flat.

Gold was discovered as early as 1845, but it wasn't until the serious gold rushes of the 1850s that the fossickers and miners moved into the area. The first major discovery occurred at **Beechworth** in 1852.

Myrtleford to the south is another town which boomed during the 1850s and waned until after World War II, when large numbers of migrants, mostly from Italy, Spain and Yugoslavia, arrived in the area and established a number of tobacco and hop farms and walnut orchards.

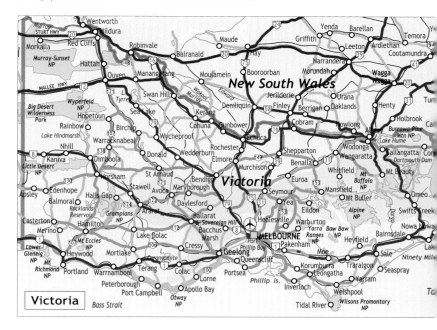

Similarly **Rutherglen**, once a gold town with a population of 25,000, is now known as the centre of viticulture. It has an annual wine festival, viticulture college and Vinegrowers Association.

Yackandandah, with its tiny population of a little over 600, is now entirely classified by the National Trust and consequently relies upon tourism to sustain it. At its height it supported 3000 miners, many of whom had travelled from the North American goldfields.

Beyond the gold towns are the Murray River towns of **Swan Hill**, **Echuca**, **Yarrawonga** and **Wodonga**.

The first paddle steamer from South Australia reached Swan Hill in 1853, and the following year port facilities were established at Wodonga. Today, the romantic riverboat past is recaptured with paddle steamer journeys down the Murray. The huge *Murray River Queen* cruises from Swan Hill to Goolwa in South Australia.

> ### GREAT OCEAN ROAD
>
> This road was completed in 1932. Before that the seaside resorts of Lorne and Apollo Bay were accessible only by narrow inland roads. The Great Ocean Road was built as a memorial to those who died in World War I and it took 15 years to complete. Everyone who worked on the road was an ex-serviceman. It starts at Torquay and skirts the coast to Peterborough. The road is one of the most magnificent coastal journeys in Australia and one of the great attractions of Victoria.

THE WESTERN DISTRICT

Along the southern coast of Victoria, from Port Phillip Bay to the South Australian border, is the western district. It includes the major regional centres of **Geelong, Portland, Port Fairy** and **Warrnambool**.

The highlight of the area is the **Great Ocean Road**, a winding coastal route which provides the traveller with superb ocean views. The **Twelve Apostles**, rock formations off the coast, are much photographed scenic wonders.

The area to the northwest of the Grampians is dry, marginal country which is good for wheat growing and sheep grazing. The Wimmera was settled by squatters in the 1830s, and settlement of the Mallee occurred about a decade later. The small, though reliable, rainfall in the Wimmera allowed for the development of wheat and sheep industries.

The towns, most of which are service centres for the pastoral areas, have tried to strengthen their fragile economic bases by establishing small, rural industries like canneries, meat-freezing works and flour mills.

Melbourne and Victoria at a Glance

Sep to **Nov** (spring) new growth brings the city alive after the cold winter. **Dec** to **Feb** (summer) warm days make exploring Victoria a joy. Melbourne is known for its changeable weather so be prepared for cool weather, even in summer.

Melbourne's **international** and **domestic airport** (Tullamarine) is 22km (14 miles) northeast of the city centre. www.melbourneair port.com.au The Tullamarine freeway makes it a fairly quick trip. **Skybus** leaves every 15 minutes for Franklin Street in the city. It provides numerous hotel drop offs. Like all big airports it caters well for the international traveller.
Many **car rental** firms have desks at both the international and domestic terminals.
Taxis are also available.
The major bus company, **Greyhound Australia**, tel: 1300 GREYHOUND, has an extensive network for interstate travellers.
Interstate train travel is easy and frequent, for information and bookings, tel: 13 2232.

Melbourne's public transport, the **METLINK**, is an integrated system incorporating bus, suburban railway and the famous **trams**. Trams are the cornerstone of the public transport system. Melbourne is laid out in a grid pattern, north–south, east–west and the trams run accordingly. The **METLINK Information Centre** will help with any queries, tel: 131 638, www.metlink melbourne.com.au Open from 07:00–20:55.
Taxis in the city are readily available and car rental firms are well represented.

Melbourne's city centre is quite small but is well catered for with excellent accommodation. The tram system makes staying just out of the central business district very easy. There are hundreds of hotels, motels and serviced apartments to choose from.
Hotel Grand Chancellor, Lonsdale St, tel: 03 9656 4000, fax: 03 9662 3479. Located inthe heart of the city, modern well appointed rooms.
Intercontinental Melbourne The Rialto, Collins St, tel: 1800 899 960. A 19th-century central hotel with style, comfort and elegance.
Stamford Plaza, Little Collins St, tel: 03 9659 1000, fax: 03 9659 0999. Luxurious s erviced apartments in the centre of the city.
Melbourne Marriott Hotel, cnr Exhibition & Lonsdale sts, tel: 03 9662 3900, fax: 03 9663 4297. Small elegant boutique hotel located in the centre of the theatre district.
Windsor Hotel, Spring St, tel: 03 9633 6002, fax: 03 9633 6001. Beautiful old-world hotel classified by the National Trust (1883), blends tradition with modern luxury.
The Westin Melbourne, 205 Collins St, tel: 03 9635 2222, fax: 03 9635 2333. Luxury hotel with every convenience to make your stay enjoyable.

BUDGET ACCOMMODATION
Batman's Hill Hotel, Spencer St, tel: 03 9614 6344, fax: 03 9614 1189. Centrally located behind Spencer Street Railway Station, excellent city hotel, priced well.
Apartments of Melbourne, tel: 03 9536 0000, fax: 03 9593 9311. Central booking office for central to suburban serviced apartments.
Punt Hill Serviced Apartments, 267 Flinders Lane, tel: 1300 662 161, fax: 03 9650 4409.
Well appointed one and two bedroom apartments; central location; reasonably priced.
Riverside Apartments, cnr Flinders St & Highlander Lane, tel: 03 9619 9199, fax: 03 9629 7582. These centrally located serviced apartments offer panoramic views over the city.
The Victoria Hotel, 215 Little Collins St, tel: 03 9653 0441, fax: 03 9650 9678. Central location with comfortable rooms and reasonably priced.

Melbourne and Victoria at a Glance

WHERE TO EAT

Melbourne is considered the culinary capital of Australia. The variety of restaurants is extraordinary. There are a number of food guides available to help the confused traveller. *Dining in Melbourne* from the Melbourne Tourism Authority describes the cuisine and includes location maps. *The Age* newspaper also produces a *Good Food Guide* for Melbourne which can be picked up at most local newsagencies. No culinary visit to Melbourne is complete without a visit to Lygon Street. There is no need to book. Just ask the taxi driver to take you to Lygon Street and then find the restaurant which suits your wallet and taste buds.

Colonial Tramcar, tel: 03 9696 4000. Enjoy Australian cuisine while travelling in a beautifully renovated tramcar.

Donovans Restaurant, St Kilda, tel: 03 9534 8221. A fun family restaurant right on the beach with menus to appeal to both adults and children.

The Looney Bin Licensed Theatre Restaurant, Spencer St, tel: 03 9329 5712.

For something completely different – good food and lots of laughing.

Becco, Crossley St, tel: 03 9663 3000. In the city centre, good food, fast service and great atmosphere.

Masani Restaurant, Drummond St, Carlton, tel: 03 9347 5610. Exceptional Italian cuisine.

Vue de Monde, Little Collins St, tel: 03 9691 3888. Elegant, with French flair.

Mekong Delta, Toorak Rd, tel: 03 9827 6833. Sophisticated dining offering authentic Vietnamese food.

TOURS AND EXCURSIONS

McCafferty's Bus & Coach Service, tel: 13 1499. Offer a large selection of coach tours around Melbourne and further afield in modern air-conditioned coaches.

City Explorer is a double-decker bus which operates hourly from Flinders St Station and calls at the main points of interest around the city.

City River Cruises, tel: 03 9650 2214. MV *Melba Star* gives the sightseer a wonderful one-hour cruise on the Yarra

River. Luncheon and dinner services are also available.

Out and About Heritage Walks, tel: 03 9656 9800. Hosted by the National Trust this is a conducted historical walk through Melbourne, including talks about the city and its architecture.

Phillip Island Nature Park, tel: 03 5951 2800 fax 03 5956 8394. Phillip Island is located 90 minutes from Melbourne and offers outstanding 'Little Penguin' viewing.

USEFUL CONTACTS

Parks Victoria, tel: 13 1963, www.parkweb.vic.gov.au Manages the state parks and gives helpful information for bushwalkers.

Information Victoria, Little Collins St, tel: 1300 36 6356. It has a large range of maps and guide books. www.information.vic.gov.au

National Trust of Victoria, Tasman Terrace, tel: 03 9656 9800. Its information centre can help travellers explore the history of Melbourne's Victorian past.

Royal Automobile Club of Victoria, Collins St, tel: 13 1955. Centrally located in the heart of the city. Offers a large selection of road maps, accommodation guides and provides helpful information to the traveller.

MELBOURNE	J	F	M	A	M	J	J	A	S	O	N	D
AVERAGE TEMP. °F	68	68	66	63	57	53	52	53	55	59	63	64
AVERAGE TEMP. °C	20	20	19	17	14	12	11	12	13	15	17	18
SEA TEMP. °F	66	66	64	64	60	59	57	55	55	57	59	63
SEA TEMP. °C	19	19	18	18	16	15	14	13	13	14	15	17
RAINFALL in	2	2	2	2	2	2	2	2	2	2.5	2.5	2
RAINFALL mm	48	48	52	58	58	50	49	51	59	68	60	59
Days of Rainfall	8	7	9	12	14	14	15	16	15	14	12	11

5
Hobart and Tasmania

Tasmania is the smallest of Australia's states, yet it is an area of great and undiscovered beauty.

The island is the most mountainous of Australia's states. Subject to extensive glaciation during the last ice age, the southern coastline, which has no settlements, is a series of rugged, inaccessible cliffs.

The centre of the island is a plateau with glacial lakes and a number of major mountains, most notably **Mount Ossa**, **Ben Lomond**, **Cradle Mountain** and **Eldon Park**. All rise above 1400m (4600ft).

Most of the island's mountainous terrain remains in its natural state, its agricultural land being concentrated along the north coast and in the valleys of the **Tamar, Derwent** and **Huon rivers**.

For decades, the apple was the symbol for the state, firstly because the island's shape is similar to an apple and secondly, because, for many Australians, apples were the only product they associated with Tasmania.

Tasmanian fauna and flora is of unique importance. The Huon pine can grow for over 2000 years. The Tasmanian devil, once an inhabitant of mainland Australia, is now restricted to the island and the Tasmanian tiger is still thought to be hiding in the state's wilderness.

HOBART

Unique among the state capitals, Hobart has a strong sense of its colonial, 19th-century heritage.

Named after Robert Hobart, Secretary of State for War and the Colonies at the time of its settlement, it is

DON'T MISS

*** **Port Arthur:** remnants of Australia's convict past.
*** **Cradle Lake:** marvellous, dramatic wilderness.
*** **Ross and Richmond:** beautifully preserved 19th-century villages.
*** **Battery Point** and **Salamanca Place:** old-world charm in Hobart.
** **The Nut at Stanley:** strange north coast outcrop.
* **Queenstown:** a moonscape produced by mining and pollution.

Opposite: *The Russell Falls Nature Walk is a half hour stroll through stands of stringybark, mountain ash and white gum.*

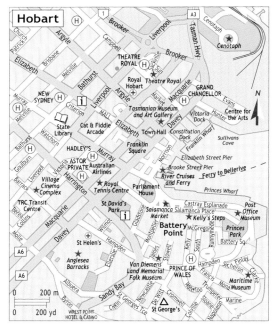

Tasmania's chief port. It is protected from the worst of the island's weather, which occurs on Tasmania's rugged west coast.

The city lies on either side of the Derwent River and is partially protected by Mount Wellington in the west and Mount Nelson to the south.

Hobart's location on the Derwent, its straggling, irregular appearance, and the distinctive old-world charm of its docklands and port have often been written about in glowing terms. The dockside warehouses at Salamanca Place are fine examples of this.

Hobart had inauspicious beginnings. Its sole *raison d'être* was to keep the French out of Australia. By 1827 it had an estimated population of 5000. In recent times, tourism to the city has increased significantly, fuelled by the establishment of Australia's first legal casino, The Wrest Point Hotel–Casino. The casino, with its distinctive 64m (210ft) high cylindrical tower, is at Sandy Bay.

Opposite: *One of Hobart's great attractions is the Royal Tasmanian Botanical Gardens which lie on the banks of the Derwent River, just beyond Government House.*

CLIMATE

Hobart has an average annual rainfall of 630mm (25in) and a temperature range from a summer monthly average of 21°C (70°F) in February, to a winter monthly average of 11°C (52°F) in July. It often snows in winter.

CITY SIGHTSEEING
The Royal Tasmanian Botanical Gardens ★★

In 1826, with the widespread agreement that Hobart Town should be the capital of Van Diemen's Land, Governor Arthur had plans drawn up for Government House and an adjoining Botanical Gardens on the banks of the Derwent. Over the next five years, plants were imported from England and over 150 native species were collected from Mount Wellington. The gardens grew progressively during the 19th century.

An excellent map and comprehensive history of the gardens is provided in the brochure *Let's Talk About The Royal Tasmanian Botanical Gardens*. It gives details about the historic Arthur Wall (built by Governor Arthur in 1829), the Rossbank Observatory site (built by Governor Franklin in 1840), the Conservatory, Rosarium, Floral Clock, Fern House and Tropical Glasshouse.

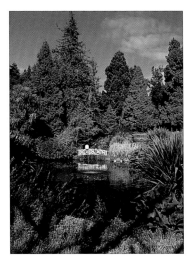

Battery Point ★★★

No other Australian city has an area to equal Battery Point. It is a very elegant 'suburb' with an extraordinary concentration of beautifully preserved 19th-century houses.

The only way to experience Battery Point is to walk up Kelly's Steps from **Salamanca Place** and start wandering through the winding streets. Battery Point gets its name from the battery of guns which were mounted on the headland in 1818.

It was around this time that building started with Stowell and Secheron House (built around 1831 and located at 21 Secheron Road) and the construction of the impressive warehouses in Salamanca Place.

By 1850, Salamanca Place and Battery Point had become the maritime focal point of the city. Sailors came from all over the world and sailors' and workers' cottages were built in an area which was already noted for its gracious Georgian mansions. In this sense, Battery Point is a unique combination of living styles. Neat, tiny cottages owned by working people stand next to mansions in a streetscape which includes roads and even 'village greens' designed to mimic the streets of rural and urban England.

The most impressive and famous building in Battery Point is **St George's Church,** built from 1836 to 1838. It is regarded as the finest Greek Revival Church in Australia.

It is fun to explore Battery Point, enjoying the sense of surprise offered by the whole area. If you want something a little more organised, the National Trust offers conducted walking tours on Saturday mornings.

HIGHLIGHTS OF BATTERY POINT

• **St George's Church:** built between 1836 and 1838, regarded as the finest Greek Revival Church in Australia with its impressive Doric portico and decorative carvings.
• **Barton Cottage:** at 72 Hampden Road built in 1837 by Captain William Wilson and now bed and breakfast accommodation.
• **Colville Cottage:** (1877) at 32 Mona Street.
• **Cromwell Cottage:** (1880) at 6 Cromwell Street.
• **Tantallon Lodge:** (1906) at 8 Mona Street.
The National Trust offers conducted walking tours on Saturday mornings.

Historic Buildings in the City

The pamphlet *Let's Talk About Hobart's Historic Buildings* concentrates on the important historic buildings and sites in the city's central business district. The visitor can see most of the important buildings by completing a circuit from the City Hall up Macquarie Street to Harrington Street then down towards Salamanca Place and back along Davey Street.

The buildings of particular note include the **Commissariat Store** (1808–10) at 40 Macquarie Street (Hobart's oldest building), the **Bond Store** (1824) behind the Commissariat, the **Tasmanian Museum and Art Gallery** (1863) and the **Town Hall**, with its impressive ballroom, which was built in 1864.

Of particular note is the **Theatre Royal** at 29 Campbell Street, which was built in 1837 and is recognised as the oldest theatre in Australia. The stage has been trod by such theatrical luminaries as Laurence Olivier and Noel Coward.

Anglesea Barracks ★★

Further up Davey Street are the **Anglesea Barracks**. Built in 1814, they are recognised as the oldest military establishment still in use in Australia. Any tour of the barracks should include the Guard House (1838), the Hospital (1818), the Military Gaol (1846), the Officers' Quarters (1814) and the Old Drill Hall (1824).

Mount Wellington ★★

Towering over the city is Mount Wellington, a dormant volcano which is 1270m (4165ft) high. On Christmas Day 1798, George Bass became the first European to climb the mountain and to enjoy the spectacular view across the Derwent River and down the D'Entrecasteaux Channel.

SALAMANCA PLACE

Every year, the victorious yacht which has led the fleet from Sydney in the Sydney–Hobart Ocean Yacht Race arrives at Salamanca Place. Each weekend, locals and visitors mingle in the excellent Salamanca Markets. And, it is at Salamanca Place that the Georgian warehouses (built between 1830 and 1850) have been converted into excellent restaurants, galleries, craft and gift shops. It is widely recognised that these are the finest dockside Georgian warehouses remaining in Australia.

It has become one of the major sites of Hobart and, over the years, it has been climbed by such famous people as Charles Darwin and the novelist Anthony Trollope who, having climbed it in 1872, rather haughtily described it as 'just enough of a mountain to give excitement to ladies and gentlemen'.

Boat Trips to the Cadburys Factory ★★

The Cruise Company's vessels depart from Brooke Street Pier, Franklin Wharf, and make their way up-river to the Cadburys factory at Claremont where, apart from the educational interest of seeing chocolate being produced, the visitor gets an opportunity to sample and purchase the product; tel: 03 6234 9294.

A number of other cruises are available which go around the harbour, down the Derwent and through the D'Entrecasteaux Channel.

Opposite: *Located on the Derwent River, Hobart retains much of its 19th-century charm. This view from Mount Nelson, with the Wrest Point Hotel–Casino in the foreground, captures the beauty of this small city.*

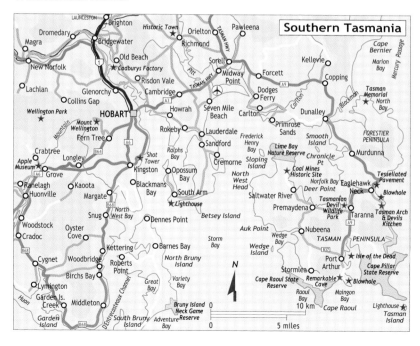

BOAT HARBOUR

Located 183km (113 miles) northwest of Launceston, Boat Harbour may well be the most beautiful place on the whole north coast of Tasmania. This charming village, located on the side of a gentle hill which tumbles down to a superb white beach with rocky headlands on either side, looks like a picture off a chocolate box or a scenic calendar. The sea is bright green and blue, the beach very clean, the surroundings delightful, and the village is sleepy and peaceful.

Opposite: *Coles Bay and Freycinet National Park, on Tasmania's east coast, offer visitors the opportunity to fish in the waters of Great Oyster Bay, to walk in the park and climb the Hazards or the mountains to the south, both of which offer marvellous views across Wine Glass Bay and out across the Tasman Sea.*

This Week in Tasmania, a free guide widely available in hotels and tourist offices in Hobart, offers an extensive overview to restaurants, hotels and motels in the city centre. The restaurants around **Constitution Dock** are essential for anyone wanting to enjoy reasonably priced and deliciously fresh seafood.

FROM HOBART TO LAUNCESTON

The most important pastoral area in Tasmania lies in the valley which has been created by the confluence of the South Esk, Macquarie and Tamar rivers. This rich, flat valley which has Launceston as its main centre, and is traversed by the main north–south road which joins Launceston and Hobart, is the most important wool- and beef-growing area in the state.

The drive from Hobart to Launceston is a rare opportunity to experience what Australia must have been like in the 19th century. Villages such as **Ross** and **Richmond** have been preserved and, although they are now the focus of the tourist industry, it is easy to appreciate their original charm with a little stretch of the imagination.

Tasmania's second major centre is **Launceston**. With a population approaching 100,000 it has retained the ambience of a large country town. Launceston is an attractive and important centre with a large number of historic buildings. The enthusiastic tourist could easily spend a day exploring the city. Of particular note are the **Gorge**, a popular swimming and picnicking location, the **Penny Royal**, a tourist attraction which includes the **Penny Royal Gunpowder Mill** and an old **tramway**, and the **harbour**.

THE NORTH AND EAST COASTS

The northwest coastal strip, running from **Smithton** and **Stanley** across to **Devonport**, is acknowledged as the best land on the island. The soils are rich and volcanic, and climatic conditions are ideal for the raising of beef and dairy cattle (the area is known for its cheeses and prime quality beef) and the growing of potatoes and peas.

The northern and northeastern coastal strip from Devonport across the estuary of the Tamar River to **Scottsdale** and **Gladstone** and around the coast to **St**

Helens and **Scamander** is heavily cropped. The area produces substantial harvests of potatoes, wheat and barley.

This entire coast is worth exploring. It has not been overdeveloped and, when the weather is good, to walk up **The Nut** at Stanley or marvel at the beauty of the windswept beaches at **Boat Harbour** (surely one of the loveliest places on the entire island) or **Penguin**, is to experience the intense beauty of this lovely region.

King Island to the northwest of Tasmania has an extraordinary reputation for dairy products. It is believed that the island's pastures have grown from seeds in mattresses washed up after shipwrecks. King Island butters, cheeses and creams are found in delicatessens on the mainland and have become a byword for quality.

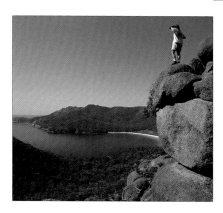

THE WEST COAST

The West Coast is wild, windy, rainy and isolated. It is a mixture of the magical and the bizarre. The whole area can be summed up by **Macquarie Harbour** and the small town of Strahan.

Strahan, on the edge of the unspoilt beauty of Macquarie Harbour, is the last outpost of civilisation on the west coast and surely one of the loneliest places on earth. The British created this place to be the ultimate penal colony. Named after Governor Lachlan Macquarie, the 50km (31 mile) long harbour opens to the sea through the narrow, eddying waters of Hells Gates and receives the waters from the **King** and **Gordon rivers**.

It was established in 1821, and closed down in 1833, when the convicts were all removed to Port Arthur on the east coast. The prisoners worked on a nearby coal seam and rowed across the harbour each day to cut down the large stands of Huon pine which edged the waterways.

It was from here that the notorious convict, Alexander Pearce, attempted to escape in 1822. Pearce and seven other convicts sought to cross the island to Hobart where

CRADLE MOUNTAIN

Located 144km (90 miles) from Launceston and 83km (50 miles) from Devonport, Cradle Mountain is the central feature of the Cradle Mountain–Lake St Clair National Park, part of Tasmania's World Heritage area. The park covers an area of 124,942ha (309,000 acres) which is characterised by a rugged, glaciated landscape with over 25 major peaks and a wide range of glacial formations – tarns, glacial lakes, moraine deposits, U-shaped valleys and water-falls. The area was glaciated during the last ice age (about 10,000 years ago) when a huge 6km (4-mile) ice cap formed and glaciers flowed from its edges, carving the landscape into dramatic shapes with their inexorable erosive powers. The park offers many superb walks.

they hoped they could catch a merchant ship and escape to some ill-defined freedom. However, they lost their way and, in the ensuing weeks, all of the escapees disappeared except for Pearce. When he was recaptured, unproven accusations of cannibalism were made against him. The following year Pearce escaped again, accompanied by another convict, Thomas Cox. Once again Pearce found himself without food and, to solve the problem, he killed and ate Cox. When he was finally recaptured Pearce admitted to eating Cox and confessed to cannibalism during his first escape. He was subsequently executed in Hobart.

The harbour remains virtually untouched. On a clear day it is like a near-perfect mirror. Its waters are stained by the brown button grass which grows on the river banks and its shores are heavily wooded. Taking a trip across the harbour and entering the **Franklin – Gordon Wild Rivers National Park** is one of the essential trips in western Tasmania.

The west coast is also a major mining area. In 1871, a man known to everyone as 'Philosopher' Smith discovered tin at Mount Bischoff. In the next decade, substantial deposits of silver were found at Zeehan, Waratah, Dundas and Farrell; copper was found at Mount Lyell and Queenstown; tin was discovered at Mount Cameron, Renison Bell and Thomas's Plains; and goldfields were established at Queenstown, Beaconsfield and along the banks of the Pieman River.

Below: *Recognised as the finest convict ruins in Australia, Port Arthur is one of Tasmania's premier tourist attractions. The historic church, which stands on the hill above the prison, is without a roof or windows.*

Queenstown, its hills stripped of timber to fire the local copper smelters and permanently denuded by the sulphurous fumes which belch from the smelters, is a surreal nightmare. Its river is polluted and it has the appearance of a deserted moonscape. Yet beyond the reaches of its devastation lie undulating hills covered in morning mist, skies heavy with the dark, low clouds which are such a distinctive part of the climate of the western coast. It is like no other place on earth and a must for those interested in seeing what pollution can do to a beautiful area.

SOUTH OF HOBART

Tasmania has become a popular retreat for people wishing to practice an alternative lifestyle. The **Huon Valley** and the rural areas around Hobart have been settled by potters, woodworkers and craftspeople who sell their wares in the gift shops in the city centre. A round trip from Hobart through Snug and Cygnet and Huonville is a reminder that there are still places on earth which have not been spoilt by modernisation and industrialisation. It is in the south of Hobart, that the bulk of the state's famous apples are grown as well as apricots and lucrative crops of oil poppies and hops.

Port Arthur ★★★

Most remarkable of all the places in Tasmania is Port Arthur. This magnificently preserved penal colony is a powerful reminder of Australia's early history. About 100km (62 miles) from Hobart, and isolated from the rest of the island by a narrow sliver of land known as Eaglehawk Neck, 12,500 of the most hardened criminals were sent to Port Arthur between 1830 and 1877. And, just to compound the misery in the area, from 1834 to 1849, a special prison for juveniles was in operation across the bay at Port Puer.

The prison at Port Arthur has been magnificently preserved and it is the best opportunity to experience Australia's convict past. The great challenge for the visitor to Port Arthur is to try to imagine what the settlement was like in the 1850s and 1860s. Anthony Trollope has left us a rather glowing description of a place which has 'the appearance of a large, well-built, clean village with various factories, breweries, and the like'. It is also hard to imagine that by the 1850s Port Arthur was a remarkably self-sufficient settlement and that the convicts were involved in industries as diverse as ship building, growing vegetables, making shoes and boots, manufacturing clothing, making bricks and cutting and processing timber.

Most visitors to Port Arthur include the ferry trip across to the **Isle of the Dead** as part of their itinerary. It became the burial place for Port Arthur residents in 1831and almost immediately was divided into free settler and convict burial grounds.

DON'T MISS – PORT ARTHUR

★★★ The Penitentiary: reputedly the largest building in Australia when it was completed in 1844.

★★★ The Isle of the Dead: burial place for Port Arthur. Over the years, a total of 1769 convicts and 180 free persons were buried on this isolated island.

★★ The Model Prison: Designed by the Royal Engineers and built with convict labour in 1848, based on the model of Pentonville Gaol in London.

★★ Hospital: substantial ruins, originally built in 1842 and once housed up to 80 ill convicts.

Hobart and Tasmania at a Glance

Sep to **Nov** (spring) Tasmania is alive with new growth and blooms. Fruit trees and spring flowers carpet the countryside. **Dec** to **Feb** (summer) long twilight evenings in ideal temperate conditions allow for extended exploration of Tasmania. Spring and summer have warm days and cool nights. Although winter can be mild it does come with rainy and unreliable weather and snow on the highlands.

Hobart's **Airport** is 26km (16 miles) east of Hobart. **Airporter Shuttle Bus** runs a pick-up and drop-off service between the airport and the city centre. **Qantas**, **Jetstar** and **Virgin Blue** have flights to Tasmania from most Australian state capitals. If you want a more leisurely journey, or want to take a car to the island, the *Spirit of Tasmania* departs nightly at 20:00 all year round. During certain peak periods (*see* www. spiritoftasmania.com.au/the ships/schedule.htm) there are also day sailings which depart at 09:00. This car ferry, which is more like a luxury cruise ship, departs from Station Pier at the northern end of Beaconsfield Pde in Melbourne and from The Esplanade in East Devonport. The journey normally takes 11 hours although the day schedule can see the ship complete the journey in 9 hours. *Spirit of Tasmania* can

also provide holiday packages. Between 30 May and 28 Aug there is one sailing a week. Between 3 Sep to 13 Dec and 20 Jan to 30 Apr there are two sailings and from 17 Dec to 19 Jan there are three sailings per week. www.spiritoftasmania. com.au tel: 1800 634 906. **Qantas**, tel: 13 1313 and **Virgin Blue**, tel: 13 6789, both operate extensive networks of domestic flights.

Car rental is the most popular form of transportation around Tasmania. Distances are short and rail services are limited. There are many car rental firms in Hobart; your hotel or motel will be able to recommend a suitable firm to meet your budget requirements.
Buses within Hobart are run by Metro and are fast and efficient. Visitors wanting to travel around Tasmania should contact the three main bus companies – Redline Coaches, Metro Tasmania and Tigerline Travel. Weekend bus services are infrequent. **Taxis** are readily available.

There are many fine hotels in Hobart itself. The island is also known for its excellent guest house and bed and breakfast accommodation.
Rydges Hotel, Argyle St, tel: 1300 857 922, fax: 03 6231 1916. Elegant surroundings in this 1850s building.

Salamanca Inn, Gladstone St, tel: 03 6223 3300, fax: 03 6223 7167. This modern hotel is integrated among the old warehouses, and is well located. It has an indoor and outdoor pool, with golf nearby.
Hotel Grand Chancellor, Davey St, tel: 03 6235 4535, fax: 03 6223 8175. First-class hotel with pool, beauty salon, health club.
Wrest Point Hotel–Casino, Sandy Bay Rd, tel: 1800 03 0611. First-class hotel and casino with riverside views.
Battery Point Guest House, 'Mandalay', McGregor St, tel: 03 6224 2111, fax: 6224 3648. Attractive converted coach house and stables.

BUDGET ACCOMMODATION
City View Motel,Montagu Bay, tel: 03 6243 8388, fax: 03 6243 8155. Panoramic views and friendly service.
Hobart Midcity Hotel, Bathurst St, tel: 03 6234 6333, fax: 03 6234 0898. Central location, low prices and modern conveniences.

Launceston
Tasmania's second-largest city, situated at the head of the Tamar River. Launceston is known as the Garden City. Accommodation is plentiful.
Colonial on Elizabeth, tel: 03 6331 6588, fax: 03 6334 2765. This beautiful 1874 building has been classified by the National Trust.

Hobart and Tasmania at a Glance

Hotel Grand Chancellor Launceston, Cameron St, tel: 03 6334 3434, fax: 03 6331 7347. Elegant, centrally located hotel with all amenities.

BUDGET ACCOMMODATION
Penny Royal Motel and Apartments, 147 Paterson St, tel: 03 6331 6699, fax: 03 6334 4282. National Trust listed motel and apartments conveniently located in Launceston.
Sandors On the Park, Brisbane St, tel: 03 6331 2055, fax: 03 6334 3910. Central location opposite city park, offering quality accommodation.
Refer to *This Week in Tasmania*, a free booklet which gives a comprehensive list of restaurants, hotels and entertainment in Hobart. It is readily available in hotels, motels and tourist information offices.

WHERE TO EAT

Restaurants are plentiful in **Hobart**. Battery Point, the area around the harbour and Salamanca Place are well known for their fine restaurants and brasseries.

Mikaku Japanese Restaurant, Salamanca Place, tel: 03 6224 0882. Japanese cuisine.
Botanical Gardens Restaurant, Queens Domain, tel: 03 6236 3088. Fine Australian cuisine in a beautiful setting with great views.
Mures Upper Deck Seafood Restaurant, Victoria Dock, tel: 03 6231 1999. This a la carte restaurant offers excellent seafood and a great view.
The Point Revolving Restaurant, Wrest Point Hotel-Casino, tel: 03 6211 1750. Fresh Tasmanian ingredients, served imaginatively.

Launceston
This Week in Tasmania provides an extensive list of restaurants in and around Launceston.
The Royal Oak, Brisbane St, tel: 03 6331 5346. Bistro-style meals served in this central hotel, dating from the 1800s.
Hallam's Waterfront Restaurant, Park St, tel: 03 6334 0554. Fresh seafood seved with flair.
Fee & Me, 190 Charles St, tel: 03 6331 3195. Award-winning restaurant serving fresh, modern Australian cuisine.

TOURS AND EXCURSIONS

Most tours and excursions are run from the Tasmanian Travel Centre, tel: 03 6230 8233, fax: 03 6224 0289. Comprehensive lists of coach, self-drive and wilderness tours are available. They will also help you plan your own tour with hotel bookings and 'must see and do' activities.
Redline Coaches, tel: 1300 36 0000. The main coach line in Tasmania has many tours throughout the state.
Naturally Tasmania Tours, tel: 03 6227 1388, fax: 03 6227 1366. For the ultimate wilderness holiday.

USEFUL CONTACTS

The Tasmanian Travel Centre, 20 Davey St, tel: 03 6230 8233, fax: 03 6224 0289. Open 08:30–17:15 week days, 09:00–17:00 weekends and holidays.
The Royal Automobile Club of Tasmania, cnr Murray and Patrick sts, tel: 03 6232 6300. Road maps and advice are part of their service – make sure you have evidence of membership of a similar organisation.
Tasmanian Parks & Wildlife Services, 134 Macquarie St, tel: 1300 135 513, www.parks.tas.gov.au A valuable source which will help the visitor explore the natural beauties of Tasmania.
Discover Tasmania, 20 Davey St, tel: 03 6230 8233, www.discovertasmania.com.au

HOBART	J	F	M	A	M	J	J	A	S	O	N	D
AVERAGE TEMP. °F	70	70	68	62	57	53	53	55	59	63	64	68
AVERAGE TEMP. °C	21	21	20	17	14	12	12	13	15	17	18	20
SEA TEMP. °F	61	62	61	59	57	55	53	52	52	55	55	59
SEA TEMP. °C	16	17	16	15	14	13	12	11	11	13	13	15
RAINFALL in	2	1.5	2	2	2	2	2	2	2	2.5	2	2
RAINFALL mm	48	40	47	52	49	56	54	52	52	64	55	57
Days of Rainfall	11	10	11	12	14	14	15	15	15	16	14	13

6. Alice Springs, Darwin and the Northern Territory

The most enduring images left with the traveller to the Northern Territory are the flatness of its terrain and the incredibly vast, underpopulated isolation of the whole region. It is hard for visitors to grasp that one can drive for hundreds of kilometres without seeing another human being.

Given the inhospitable nature of the terrain it is hardly surprising that the Territory has a population of 213,800 (March 2007) spread over an area of 1,346,200km² (520,000 sq miles). Thus, while larger than every Australian state except Queensland and Western Australia, it has a total population only slightly larger than that of Hobart in Tasmania.

The history of white settlement in the territory began in 1861–62, when John McDouall Stuart crossed the country from south to north. The subsequent route for the **Overland Telegraph Line** was devised using Stuart's maps, journals and other reference matter.

In turn, the repeater stations which were established along the Overland Telegraph route became the first communities in the Territory. The pastoralists soon compounded this by using the Telegraph Line as their chief stock route. To improve the water supply along the track, bores were sunk and, as a natural result of this activity, often where these bores were sunk a small community quickly developed.

The Northern Territory is still the '**outback**' and the people still have a pioneering spirit which has long departed from the urban southeast of the continent.

DON'T MISS

*** Uluru and Kata Tjuta: spectacular rock formations.
*** Kakadu: a vast wilderness area of tropical savanna.
*** Katherine Gorge: dramatically beautiful.
*** Litchfield Park: waterfalls and swimming holes.
*** Kings Canyon and **MacDonnell Range:** spectacular gorges and scenery.
** Arltunga: a mining ghost town in the desert.
** The Devils Marbles: unusual eroded boulders south of Tennant Creek.

Opposite: *Darwin is a tropical city and its sunsets are a reminder of that intense climatic beauty.*

CLIMATE

The Northern Territory's climate ranges from near-monsoonal at the Top End to typical desert continentality (hot days and very cold nights) around Alice Springs and Uluru. The Top End divides its seasons into 'wet' (Oct to Mar) and 'dry'. In the centre it is common for temperatures to fall below freezing at night-time.

ALICE SPRINGS

The second-largest town in the Northern Territory, Alice Springs has a population of 23,892 (2006 census). Recognised as the '**Centre of Australia**' it owes its modern popularity to a booming tourist industry which brings people to '**The Alice**' to explore the beauty of **The Centre**, particularly the magnificent MacDonnell Range, or to head off to **Uluru** (Ayers Rock) and **Kata Tjuta** (The Olgas) which lie to the southwest.

Alice Springs is 576m (1900ft) above sea level and lies on the often dry Todd River. The springs, after which the town is named, lie to the northeast of the town and were discovered in 1871 by the team building the Overland Telegraph Line.

Prior to the arrival of Europeans, the area had been the home of the Aranda Aborigines who had been living in the area for at least 10,000 years.

The Old Telegraph Station which was built at Alice Springs in 1871–72 was the first European building constructed in Central Australia. The station was closed in 1932 and is now open for inspection. Built of local stone, it consisted of the postmaster's residence, an observatory and store room, the telegraph room and barracks. It lies 3km (2 miles) to the north of the town. There are guided

tours each morning at 10:00. The town has a vast number of attractions for the visitor. A good starting point is **Anzac Hill,** which offers a 360° panoramic view of Alice Springs and its environs.

Adelaide House in Todd Mall was designed and built by John Flynn and was the first Alice Springs Hospital. The idea for a hospital was originally suggested by Sister Finlayson who arrived in the Centre in 1915 and was horrified to find that seriously ill patients had to be transferred by cart or wagon to Oodnadatta, which lies over 600km (373 miles) away.

On the corner of Todd and Parsons streets is the **Flynn Memorial Church**, built in honour of the late John Flynn who established the Flying Doctor Service. Today, the **Royal Flying Doctor Base** can be inspected at the southern end of Hartley Street.

In the **Old Pioneer Cemetery** there is a dramatic gravestone depicting a wizened old miner panning for gold. This is the last burial place for Harold Lasseter who believed he had found reefs which contained vast amounts of gold in Central Australia.

The locals have gone to some trouble to achieve fame through unusual tourist attractions. The famous **Henley-on-Todd Regatta**, held every August, is notable as a race along a dry river bed, and the **Bangtail Muster** in May is an occasion when numerous humorous floats parade down the main street.

AROUND ALICE SPRINGS

Simpsons Gap National Park is located just 8km (5 miles) west of Alice Springs on Larapinta Drive and is a 30,950ha (76,500-acre) park designed to preserve a piece of typical MacDonnell Range landscape. The waterholes, the ghost and red river gums, and the tame rock wallabies are particular attractions.

Henbury Meteorite Conservation Park lies 145km (90 miles) south of Alice Springs on the Stuart Highway. It is the site of a large number of meteorite craters. Scientists estimate that a meteorite crashed into the area about 7400 years ago.

Ewaninga Rock Carvings Reserve is 35km (22 miles) south of Alice Springs and contains some of the most interesting and impressive Aboriginal rock carvings in the Northern Territory. Unfortunately, their meanings have been lost over time.

Standley Chasm is one of the most popular tourist attractions around Alice Springs. Located 50km (31 miles) west of The Alice off Larapinta Drive it is a steep gorge within the MacDonnell Range. The walk into the chasm takes about 20 minutes.

FLYNN OF THE INLAND

The Northern Territory has numerous memorials to the pioneering work of **John Flynn**, known as Flynn of the Inland. A Presbyterian minister, he spent 39 years of his life working among the people of the outback. He built nursing homes, established welfare centres and in 1928, founded the **Australian Inland Mission Aerial Medical Service** which used the pedal wireless to establish communication with outlying stations and properties. It eventually became the **Royal Flying Doctor service**. Flynn is remembered outside Alice Springs with a monument which includes a boulder from the Devils Marbles.

Opposite: *The story of the early history of Central Australia would not be complete without mention of the Afghan camel drivers who helped to open up the wilderness. Today, the distant relatives of those early camels run wild or are bred at camel farms in the region. The farms offer interesting rides and longer safaris for those who are prepared to brave the back of a camel.*

Above: *The most popular of the many gorges in the MacDonnell Range is Standley Chasm, located 50km (31 miles) west of Alice Springs. The walk into the chasm takes about 20 minutes and, for those wishing to photograph the gorge in all its spectacular beauty, the best time is at noon when the sun strikes the walls on both sides of the chasm.*

ULURU

Uluru (previously known as Ayers Rock) is a huge monolith – 862.5m (2850ft) above sea level and 1395km (865 miles) south of Darwin. It rises 348m (1142ft) above the surrounding countryside. It has an area of 3.33km² (1.29 sq miles) and a circumference of 9.4km (5.9 miles).

Uluru and Kata Tjuta ★★★

In the language of the local Aborigines 'Uluru' is simply a place name which is applied to both the rock and to the waterhole on top of the rock.

There is some scientific disagreement about the origins of Uluru. The most widely held theory is that both Uluru and Kata Tjuta are remnants of a vast sedimentary bed which was laid down some 600 million years ago. The bed was tilted so that Uluru now protrudes at an angle of up to 85°. The rock is actually grey but is covered with a distinctive red iron-oxide coating.

In 1985, the title to the rock was handed back to the traditional custodians who, in turn, granted the Australian National Parks and Wildlife Service a 99-year lease on the park. Today, over 30 local Aborigines work in the park and the Board of Management is dominated by the traditional owners.

The caves around the base of the rock abound with hundreds of paintings which depict Aboriginal life. The caves to the left of the car park have quite a lot of interesting paintings and can be reached by an easy 10-minute walk around the base of the rock.

The decision to climb Uluru is one which should be based on fitness (it is only suitable for healthy people) and one's level of respect for the Aboriginal notion that this is a sacred site. The traditional custodians have resigned themselves to the inevitable despoliation of the rock, and climbing Uluru contributes to its despoliation.

The best time to see Uluru is at sunrise when there are less crowds. Sunset is a more convenient time, but there are literally hundreds of people jockeying for position in the sunset viewing area.

To the north lie the 36 smaller monoliths known collectively as Kata Tjuta. The highest rises to 546m (1790ft). Kata Tjuta is spread across an area of some 3500ha (8648 acres) and the distance around the group is approximately 22km (14 miles). It is thought that Kata Tjuta may have once been one gigantic monolith many times the size of Uluru. Millions of years of erosion have reduced the single monolith to a series of smaller ones.

Left: *Uluru is one of the wonders of central Australia. The best time to see it is at sunrise when the light touches the vast rock and, slowly, its colour changes.*
Below: *The decision to climb Uluru is one which should be based on fitness and the visitor's level of respect for the Aboriginal notion that this is a sacred site. It is interesting to note that the average tourist stays at Uluru for 1.6 days and only 10% of all tourists actually climb the rock. There are signs around the rock which discourage climbing.*

Kata Tjuta is noted for its engravings and its geometric rock piles. Both the engravings and the geometric rock piles are believed to have been created by the Spirit Ancestor during the Dreamtime.

Kings Canyon ★★★

There is little doubt that Kings Canyon is one of the most beautiful sites in the whole of the centre. To be seen properly, however, visitors should plan to spend at least a day and, if fit and well prepared, do both the Canyon and the Creek walks.

The short Creek Walk is about 1.5km (one mile) and takes about an hour to return. It meanders up the centre of the canyon to a lookout point on the left-hand side of the valley, which affords a view of the sheer cliff face at the end of the canyon.

The Canyon Walk is a magnificent trek through the domes on the top of the canyon, with excellent views down the canyon from the walls at the top. The National Park rangers have estimated that this walk will take around four hours (and that's at a leisurely but sensible pace). The central attraction of this walk is the 'Lost City' a magnificent series of weathered buttresses of rock which look like the long-lost ruins of an ancient city or a moonscape.

There is also a valley known as the 'Garden of Eden' which has clumps of palm trees growing around a quiet and beautiful waterhole.

THE TOP END
Darwin ★★

The climate of warm days in winter and the long hot wet from late October to March, is monsoonal and the vegetation is typical tropical savannah woodland.

The area's prosperity has relied on Darwin's importance as a port, the cattle industry, and the mineral wealth which over the years has changed from gold to uranium. Today, it is increasingly geared to tourism, ranging from visiting places of natural beauty like Kakadu National Park and Litchfield Park to inspecting the museums, historic buildings and settlements which are reminders of the Top End's past.

KAKADU NATIONAL PARK BIRDS AND WILDLIFE

As you enter the park on the Arnhem Highway the first place you will come to is the **Mamakala Observation Point**, a shaded platform from where the visitor can observe the edge of a wetlands lake with its rich variety of birdlife. **The Yellow Waters Billabong** is one of the most famous wildlife areas within the park. The accommodation at the Cooinda Motel gives access to the walks along the river, and the regular boat trips provide an opportunity to see birds, feral buffalos and crocodiles in their native habitat.

1. Performing Arts Centre
2. Beaufort Darwin Centre
3. Leichhardt Memorial
4. Old Admiralty House
5. Overland Telegraph Mem.
6. Government House
7. Browns Mart
8. Tree of Knowledge
9. Civic Centre
10. Chinese Temple
11. Deckchair Cinema
12. Stokes Hill
13. Fort Hill

Darwin

Darwin is a typical tropical township with a shopping mall and a few historical buildings that survived the three cyclones which have devastated the city.

To the south of Darwin there are a number of tourist attractions. On the Stuart Highway is **Darwin Crocodile Farm** where people can watch crocodiles being fed; on the road to Kakadu there is **Reptile World** with its hundreds of species of snakes and lizards; and then there are the boat trips down the muddy waters of the Alligator and Adelaide rivers to see saltwater crocodiles sun-basking in the mud.

The natural highlights of the Top End include the waterfalls (particularly Wangi Falls and the Florence Falls in Litchfield Park) which tumble across the escarpments, the fascinating magnetic anthills, the billabongs and vast wetlands with their myriad bird life, and the beautiful tropical sunsets and thunderstorms.

Kakadu National Park ★★★

One of the highlights of the Top End is Kakadu National Park. Listed by the World Heritage, it is now one of the most important wilderness regions in Australia covering an area of 1,307,300ha (3,230,000 acres).

Bounded to the north by Van Diemen Gulf, and to the east and west by the Wild Man and East Alligator rivers, Kakadu gained international publicity when it featured prominently in the first two *Crocodile Dundee* movies.

> ### ABORIGINAL ART IN KAKADU
>
> ★★★ **Ubirr** is an Aboriginal rock art site with international status. There are ranger talks daily at the Main Gallery at 09:00 and 17:15, on the Rainbow Serpent at 09:50 and 16:30, at the Namarrkan Sisters at 10:50 and at the Lookout for "A floodplain overview" at 17:50.
> ★★★ At **Nourlangie Rock**, located south of Jabiru, there are over 100 sacred sites, some of them are designated sacred–dangerous (and therefore not open to the public). The area has a number of cave sites and there is evidence of quarries where the local Aborigines made their stone implements.

Opposite: *Darwin's popular East Point Reserve lies at the northern end of Fannie Bay. It is an ideal vantage point for visitors to look back across the bay towards the city.*
Left: *In 1872, Darwin's Government House, a seven-gabled house which overlooks Darwin Harbour, was built. It was rebuilt in the 1880s and is now known as the 'House of Seven Gables'. The house with its magnificent tropical garden is surrounded by a white fence.*

MATARANKA AND THE 'NEVER-NEVER'

423km (263 miles) south of Darwin and 107km (66 miles) south of Katherine is Mataranka, a small, 4ha (10-acre) park with a superb thermal pool and stands of cabbage tree palms and paperbarks. Owned and operated as the Mataranka Homestead Tourist Resort, this is a popular stopover and picnic spot for visitors to the region. The resort is near the site of Elsey Station, the subject of Jeannie Gunn's enormously popular auto-biographical novel *We of the Never-Never*.

The park contains over 1000 plant species, a quarter of all the freshwater fish species found in Australia, and over one-third of all the bird species. Add to this the thousands of insects and the park is a reminder that the tropics are the breeding ground for the whole planet.

Katherine and the Never Never ★★★

If there is a region of the Northern Territory which is close to climatic perfection it would have to be the fertile and beautiful area around Katherine.

Positioned far enough south to avoid the worst ex-cesses of 'the wet', and far enough north to avoid the harshness of the centre's desert continentality, the Katherine area has extensive beef cattle holdings, mineral wealth which exists from Pine Creek north to Kakadu National Park, and a burgeoning tourist industry.

The region stretches from the drier areas of Victoria Downs and Timber Creek to the mangrove swamps of the Gulf coast near Roper Bar. This area is flat, with the excep-tion of the gorges in the Katherine region and the hilly country around Pine Creek, and covered with vegetation

from tropical savannah to tropical woodland.

It has vast cattle stations which can often be up to 810,000ha (2 million acres) with herds of 40–50,000 head. At one time Victoria Downs Station was the largest cattle station in the world.

With the beauty of the Katherine Gorge, the large number of excellent swim-ming holes, the limestone formations which have pro-duced Cutta Cutta Caves, the hot springs at Mataranka and Douglas Hot Springs, and the rich variety of fauna

Around Darwin

and flora (including the ubiquitous ant hills), the area offers visitors a range of delights.

The Barkly Tablelands ★★

Covering some 130,000km² (50,000 sq miles), the Barkly Tablelands area spreads from northwestern Queensland into the Northern Territory.

This is a flat cattle-raising area with few attractions and consequently little to interest the traveller.

The distances through the Barkly Tablelands are vast and very monotonous. There are only three places of real interest – **Tennant Creek**, the mining settlement with its unusual buildings and interesting history; the **Daly Waters Pub** which is a genuine piece of outback history; and the **Newcastle Waters Station,** which offers a fascinating insight into the life of the drovers and the hardships of living in the Territory in the 1920s and 1930s.

Opposite: *Kakadu National Park, apart from a few small areas, is flat tropical savannah woodland with low-lying rocky outcrops. It is not, as many people think, tropical rainforest. It has been World Heritage listed because of its importance as a wetlands area, not because of its tropical splendour. Near this rocky outcrop are some of the most dramatic examples of Aboriginal rock art to be seen in Australia.*

Alice Springs, Darwin and the Northern Territory at a Glance

BEST TIMES TO VISIT

The Northern Territory thinks in terms of dry and wet. **Apr** to **Sep** is the dry season. The climate is temperate and roads are accessible. During the monsoonal 'wet' season (which starts in late Oct and continues through to Mar) all the dirt roads are closed. The only way to see Kakadu's spectacular **Jim Jim Falls** in the wet is by helicopter or aeroplane. The weather around the centre is classic desert continentality. Thus, around **Uluru** and **Alice Springs** it is quite common to get temperatures rising to 40°C (104°F) during the day and dropping below 0°C (32°F) at night. Equally, the small rainfall produces a dryness which means that if you intend walking you need to take water to prevent dehydration.

GETTING THERE

Darwin's **international airport** is 6km (4 miles) from the city centre. The **airport shuttle bus** will pick up or drop off almost anywhere in the city; book a day ahead when leaving Darwin, tel: 1800 35 8945. **Taxis** are available and the major car rental firms have desks at the airport. The major bus company, **McCafferty's Bus & Coach Service**, tel: 13 1499, runs services from Darwin to Alice Springs, Tennant Creek and Mount Isa.
Alice Springs
Alice Springs' new airport is 14km (8 miles) south of town.

An airport **shuttle bus** meets all flights and takes passengers to city accommodation and the railway station. Major **car rental** firms have desks at the airport.
Darwin has an efficient local **bus service.** The city terminal is located at Harry Chan Ave, tel: 08 8924 7666.
The Tour Tub does a circuit of the city and stops at major places of interest. Darwin is well serviced by taxis and car rental firms.

GETTING AROUND

The Northern Territory has very little public transport and it is therefore advisable to plan visits which include transportation to the major destinations. Although it is a rather vast area, the only towns of any size are Darwin, Alice Springs, Tennant Creek and Katherine.

Alice Springs
There is a limited public transport system for the town but Alice Springs is very compact and getting around on foot is easy.

WHERE TO STAY

Darwin
Crowne Plaza Darwin, 32 Mitchell St, tel: 1800 669 562, fax: 08 8981 1765. Modern and sophisticated five-star hotel.
Holiday Inn Darwin, 122 The Esplanade, tel: 1800 669 562, fax: 08 8981 5701. This luxury hotel is centrally located,

known for its fine service.
Darwin Central Hotel, 21 Knuckey St, tel: 08 8944 9000, fax: 08 8944 9100. Luxury hotel in Darwin.

BUDGET ACCOMMODATION
Comfort Inn Asti Darwin, cnr Smith St and Packard Place, tel: 08 8981 8200, fax: 08 8981 8038. Quiet location; five-minute walk to the city centre; reasonably priced.
Flag Poinciana Inn, cnr Mitchell & McLachlan Streets, tel: 08 8981 8111, fax: 08 8941 2440. Convenient location; well appointed at a reasonable price.

Alice Springs
Alice Springs Resort, Stott Terrace, tel: 02 8296 8010, fax: 02 9299 2103. Offers resort-type accommodation from family to deluxe.
Lasseters Hotel Casino, Barrett Drive, tel: 08 8950 7777, fax: 08 8953 1680. Luxury hotel attached to the Alice Springs Casino facility.
Crowne Plaza Alice Springs, Barrett Drive, tel: 1800 669 562, fax: 08 8952 3822. Luxury resort accommodation situated at the base of the MacDonnell Range.

BUDGET ACCOMMODATION
Desert Palms Resort, 74 Barrett Drive, tel: 08 8952 5977, fax: 08 8953 4179. Well-appointed motel; centrally located.

Alice Springs, Darwin and the Northern Territory at a Glance

Uluru (Ayers Rock)

Ayers Rock Resort is managed by the **Voyages Group**. Contact them toll free in Australia on 1300 13 4044 or try www.ayersrockresort.com.au The resort is a large well-designed complex that can cater for any budget. **Sails in the Desert** offers luxury accommodation, while **Desert Gardens** is standard family accommodation. **Outback Pioneer Hotel and Lodge** is simple, clean and low cost and there is also the **Ayers Rock Campground**.

WHERE TO EAT

The NT Tourist Bureau puts out a free magazine with an up-to-date list of restaurants.

Darwin

Dragon Court, Gilruth Ave, Mindil Beach, tel: 08 8943 8888. Good quality chinese restaurant.
The Noodle House, Knuckney St, tel: 08 8941 1742. Wok cooking at its best.
Crustaceans on the Wharf, Stokes Hill Wharf, tel: 08 8981 8658. Popular restaurant; fresh seafood daily.
Seafood on Cullen, Marina Blvd, Cullen Bay, tel: 08 8981

4666. Friendly dining with views over the Cullen Bay.

Alice Springs

Bojangle's Bush Bistro, Todd St, tel: 08 8952 2873. Cheerful restaurant with long bar and live entertainment
Overlanders Steakhouse, Hartley St, tel: 08 8952 2159. Steakhouse with real outback atmosphere.
Sport & Café Restaurant, Todd Mall, tel: 08 8953 0935. Gourmet cooking, elegant surrounds make this an oasis.
Red Centre Dreaming Dinner & Cultural Show, Stuart Hwy, tel: 08 8950 5555. A wonderful outback experience that combines a good three course meal with a cultural show.

TOURS AND EXCURSIONS

Darwin

McCafferty's Bus & Coach Service, tel: 13 1499. Offers a range of tours, 24hr booking.
Kakadu 4-wheel-drive Safaris, tel: 08 8983 1334. A three-day action-packed four-wheel-drive adventure. Both exciting and informative.
Adventure Tours Australia, tel: 1300 654 604, overseas: 61 8 8132 8230. All inclusive tours

take you to interesting locations around the Top End.

Alice Springs

McCafferty's Bus & Coach Service, tel: 13 1499. Offer an extensive range of coach tours.
Frontier Camel Tours, tel: 08 8953 0444, fax: 08 8955 5015. A 3–4 hour adventure which includes a camel ride and an evening meal of bush tucker starting at 16:00 in winter and 17:00 in summer.
Palm Valley Tours, tel: 08 8952 0022, fax: 08 8952 0033. A variety of outback tours.
Ballooning Down Under, tel: 08 8952 8816 or 1800 809 790. Enjoy the beauties of the outback at dawn. The flight concludes with breakfast.

USEFUL CONTACTS

Northern Gateway Holidays, McMinn St, Darwin, tel: 08 8941 1394, www.northern gateway.com.au Travel advisory and booking office specialising in the Northern Territory.
Kakadu National Park, tel: 08 8920 1302, www.environ ment.gov.au/parks/kakadu
Uluru – Kata Tjuta National Park, 08 8956 3138, www.environment.gov.au/parks/uluru

ALICE SPRINGS	J	F	M	A	M	J	J	A	S	O	N	D
AVERAGE TEMP. °F	84	82	78	68	59	55	53	57	64	73	78	82
AVERAGE TEMP. °C	29	28	26	20	15	13	12	14	18	23	26	28
RAINFALL in	1	1.5	1.5	1	1	1	1	0.5	0	1	1	1.5
RAINFALL mm	36	41	38	14	19	14	16	11	9	21	26	37
Days of Rainfall	5	5	3	2	3	3	3	2	2	5	5	5

7
Adelaide and South Australia

South Australia is Australia's third-largest state. It covers a total of 984,400km² (380,000 sq miles) of which just under half is nothing more than deserts of saltbush, mulga and seemingly endless sand dunes and flat, waterless lakes.

As a result, over 75% of the population live in Adelaide, and the rest are scattered in small settlements along the Murray River and around the coastline of Gulf St Vincent and Spencer Gulf.

The region which is deemed to be of the greatest economic value covers about 215,000km² (83,000 sq miles) in the south and southeast of the state. This is the area of the Flinders and Mount Lofty ranges, the Eyre, Yorke and Fleurieu peninsulas, and the Coorong and the Murray River valley.

Most of this area experiences cold, moist winters and dry hot summers. These conditions, which exist upon the coast, weaken further inland, eventually degenerating into areas of low rainfall and high temperatures.

History has been kind to South Australia. The two events – convict transportation and the gold rushes – which did so much to define the nature and character of most of Australia, are missing from the state's early historical accounts.

In 1829, Edward Gibbon Wakefield proposed a scheme for careful and systematic colonisation. A fleet of eight ships captained by John Hindmarsh left England and arrived at Holdfast Bay on 28 December 1836. The land near the site of modern-day Adelaide had been

DON'T MISS

*** Mount Gambier's Blue Lake: a volcanic lake.
** The Adelaide Hills: towns nestling behind Adelaide.
*** The Flinders Ranges: dramatic desert scenery.
*** Nullarbor cliffs: dramatic cliffs on the edge of the Nullarbor Plain.
** Hahndorf: a piece of Germany in Australia.
** The Barossa Valley: premier wine-producing area.
** Port Lincoln: where tuna fishermen reap rich harvests from the southern oceans.

Opposite: *Adelaide's St Peters Church is one of the reasons the city is called 'City of Churches'.*

CLIMATE

Adelaide enjoys a typically Mediterranean climate with an average rainfall of 560mm (22in) and a temperature range from 12°C (54°F) in Jul to 23°C (73°F) in Feb. Most of the rain falls in the winter and summer can become very hot and dry.

Opposite: *The Torrens River, the Festival Centre, the small modern city in the background and the boats for hire on the river banks are just some of the attractions that draw visitors to Adelaide.*

surveyed and sold by March 1837, but surveys of country areas were delayed and property speculation became the colony's main industry. By 1840, only three years after first settlement, the colony had a population of 14,000 free settlers but was totally bankrupt.

Out of these unlikely origins, South Australia has managed to extricate itself so that now it is recognised as the centre of Australia's wine industry, a vital part of the nation's rich mineral base, an important area of secondary industry, and a state of great charm and beauty.

ADELAIDE

Spread out on either side of the Torrens River on the plain between Gulf St Vincent and the Mount Lofty Range lies Adelaide, an overgrown country town laid out in a series of easy-to-follow grids. Dubbed 'the city of churches' it is more the serenity of the city than the actual number of churches which inspires this notion of religious commitment.

A Mediterranean-style city, Adelaide is designed for outdoor living. Its shopping malls, beautiful parks and the Torrens River flowing slowly through its centre are all conducive to leisurely walks and picnics.

During the last half century Adelaide has sprawled. Its suburbs now spread for nearly 40km (25 miles) to the south, reaching almost to the McLaren Vale wine-growing area. To the east they nestle into the Adelaide Hills and, to the north, they spill into the industrialised sprawl of Elizabeth and Salisbury.

City Sightseeing

Any visit to Adelaide is really a three-pronged exercise. There are the historic buildings, the parks and malls, and the interesting outlying suburbs.

Art Gallery ★★

Located in North Terrace, the Art Gallery of South Australia is open from 10:00 to 17:00 daily. Admission is free. It is known for its wide range of early prints and drawings of colonial Australia. It also has excellent displays of Southeast Asian ceramics.

Ayers House ★★

Situated at 288 North Terrace, Ayers House is an elegant Regency building which was built in 1846 for William Paxton. Today, the house, which has been restored by the South Australian Government, houses the National Trust of South Australia.

THE ADELAIDE HILLS

Once an area of small-scale farming, milling and cool summer retreats, the Adelaide Hills are now one of South Australia's most popular tourist destinations. At various times, it has supported mixed farming, sheep and cattle, vineyards, flour mills, commercial vegetable gardens and a rich diversity of arts and crafts. The small villages – Birdwood, Cudlee Creek, Blackwood, Clarendon, Glen Osmond, Gumeracha, Hahndorf, Lobethal, Mount Barker – are attractive and intimate.

Botanic Gardens ★★★

This historic garden was established in 1855, and is one of the most delightful in Australia. Open Monday to Friday from 08:00 to sunset, and on weekends from 09:00 to sunset, it is a cool escape beside the Torrens River. Among the most impressive displays are the Museum of Economic Botany, a new glasshouse, a magnificent wisteria arbour and an avenue of Moreton Bay figs which were originally planted in 1866. Of equal interest is the State Herbarium, an institute for research which boasts a collection of more than half a million dried plants from all over the world.

Festival Centre ★★

An impressive arts complex on the banks of the Torrens River, the Festival Centre comprises a drama and lyric theatre, an open-air amphitheatre, an experimental theatre and a multipurpose concert hall. The venue for the biennial Adelaide Arts Festival, the complex offers a range of interesting cultural activities throughout the year.

Holy Trinity Church ★

Located at 87 North Terrace, this Anglican church is known as 'The pioneer church of South Australia'. The foundation stone was laid by Governor Hindmarsh in 1838. It was rebuilt and enlarged in 1844, and again in 1888. The church clock was made by Vulliamy, the clockmaker to King William IV and Queen Adelaide.

Tandanya ★

Home of the National Aboriginal Cultural Institute, Tandanya is located in the East End Precinct of the city. It provides a unique opportunity for visitors to experience living Aboriginal culture in its historic context.

Visitors will also want to explore the Rundle Mall and perhaps experience Hindley Street at night, Adelaide's answer to Sydney's Kings Cross. Further information can be obtained at the city's Information Centre on the corner of Rundle Mall and King William Street, tel: 8203 7611.

SUBURBAN ADELAIDE
Glenelg ★★

No visit to Adelaide is complete without the 10km (6-mile) tram ride to Glenelg. Today it is a typical seaside resort. Historically, it was where Adelaide really started.

Of particular historic interest is the Old Gum Tree where, on 28 December 1836, Governor Hindmarsh reputedly read the proclamation declaring South Australia a British colony.

A replica of HMS *Buffalo*, the ship in which Governor Hindmarsh arrived, is located north of the centre of Glenelg. It is used as a restaurant.

The Adelaide Hills ★★

Once an area of small-scale farming, milling and cool summer retreats, the Adelaide Hills are now one of South Australia's most popular tourist destinations. Correctly known as the **Mount Lofty Range** the area, at various times, has supported mixed farming, sheep and cattle, vineyards, flour mills, commercial vegetable gardens and a rich diversity of arts and crafts.

The streams which flow through the hills were ideal sources of power for the establishment of flour mills. At Birdwood, the famous Murray riverboat pioneer and adventurer, Captain William Randell, built a mill in 1852; at **Bridgewater** the old flour mill is now used in the production of wines; and between Hahndorf and Mount Barker stands another disused mill. Randell's

---

ADELAIDE ZOO

Located on the banks of the Torrens River and surrounded by the city's superb Botanic Gardens, the zoo is over 100 years old. Inevitably this means that its 1500 exotic and native mammals, birds and reptiles are housed in a setting characterised by Victorian elegance. Its popular attractions include an Australian Wetlands Exhibit, a walk-through Australian Rainforest Exhibit and a re-creation of Seal Bay on Kangaroo Island. The zoo prides itself on its collection of endangered species which include the golden-lion tamarin, red panda, scimitar-horned oryx and Persian leopard. It is open from 09:30 to 17:00.

ADELAIDE'S MUSEUMS

Migration Museum: offers a rare and interesting overview of Australia's migration programmes since the early 19th century.
South Australian Museum: contains five floors of natural and cultural history with particular emphasis on the fossils, animals and minerals of South Australia.
South Australian Maritime Museum: located at 126 Lipson Street in Port Adelaide and open from 10:00–17:00 daily, this museum extends across a number of historic sites including the 1869 lighthouse, and 1850s bond store.

mill is now home to the National Motor Museum.

Also found among the Adelaide Hills are a number of tourist attractions. At Kersbrook there is a trout farm; Springfield has 'Carrick Hill', the former home of Sir Edward and Lady Hayward, on display; and Norton Summit boasts another vice-regal summer retreat.

The centrepiece of the whole area is, however, **Hahndorf** – the oldest surviving German settlement in Australia. The Germans, who settled in Hahndorf in 1840, were endlessly energetic and did much to establish milling, orchards and commercial vegetable growing in the area. Equally, they retained their cultural heritage so that today, Hahndorf still looks like a transported piece of Germany. It is the home of craftsmen, European-style bakeries, art galleries, and shops where German sausages and condiments can be purchased.

Below: *South Australia is famous for its grape growing and wine production. The Barossa Valley Wine Festival is held every two years and, apart from sampling the wines, one of the fun things to try is the ancient grape-crushing method.*

The Barossa Valley ★★

An important part of any visit to South Australia is a journey to the state's vineyards (located conveniently close to Adelaide) and an opportunity to taste some of the Barossa Valley's exceptional wines. The Australian wine industry established its reputation for quality in the valleys of South Australia.

South Australians recognise 13 major wine areas, which produce wines ranging from cheap cask wines to award-winning vintages. South Australian vineyards produce every kind of wine from reds to whites, champagnes, after-dinner sauternes, ports and sherries.

Undoubtedly, the most famous wine-growing area in South Australia is the **Barossa Valley** where, ever since the German immigrants arrived in the 1840s, wine has been grown commercially. The valley is small – 30km (18 miles) long and 8km (5 miles) wide – but within the area the soils, temperatures and rainfall vary so much that a wide variety of excellent wines are produced. Over 100km (62 miles) to the north of the Barossa Valley, and nestled into the Mount Lofty Range, is the Clare Valley. Vineyards were introduced into this area in 1848, by the Austrian Jesuit priest, Father Aloysius Kranewitter. The area produces about 4% of the Australian grape crop and is home to such wineries as Stanley Leasingham, Quelltaler, Taylors and Fareham Estate.

Located 39km (24 miles) south of Adelaide is the outstanding wine growing area surrounding the town of McLaren Vale. Highlights include the vineyards at Hardy's at Reynella, Coriole, D'Arenberg, Wirra Wirra, Maxwell and Fox Creek. SA Tourism have an excellent 180-page free booklet titled *South Australian Secrets: A Glove Box Guide to South Australia's Wine Country* which offers detailed information on every winery in the region.

AROUND THE STATE

South Australia offers the visitor some of the country's most interesting scenery, ranging from the extraordinary desert which lies to the north of Port Augusta through the beautiful Flinders Range to the coastal beaches and the dramatic coastline around Port Lincoln and across to the spectacular cliffs at the edge of the Nullarbor.

The highlights include **Kangaroo Island**, at the entrance of Gulf St Vincent, which is the third-largest island off the Australian coast. It is recognised, particularly by

Opposite above: *While most of South Australia is desert, areas such as the rich grazing lands around the historic town of Penola in the state's southeast are ideal for the breeding of Hereford cattle.*

Below: *The Flinders Range is spectacular. Wilpena Pound, the ghost gums beside the roads, the wilderness and the loneliness of the area, all help to make this an area which is uniquely beautiful and uniquely Australian.*

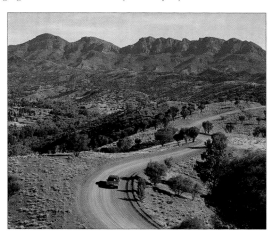

Right: *Nullarbor, from the Latin words 'nullus arbor', means 'no trees'. Today, the Nullarbor Plain refers to all the flatlands lying to the north of the Great Australian Bight. The Eyre Highway runs for hundreds of kilometres through countryside where there is nothing other than dry stunted grasses and low-lying hardy desert bushes. The effect is both monotonous and mesmerising.*

KANGAROO ISLAND

Kangaroo Island, at the entrance of Gulf St Vincent, is the third-largest island off the Australian coast. It is 145km (90 miles) long and 55km (34 miles) at its widest point. **Reeves Point**, near the island's main town of Kingscote, is the site of South Australia's first Post Office and oldest cemetery. It is, by any measure, wild and beautiful. One early Australian writer's description of it was that, 'The southern coast of the island is bold, rock-bound and inaccessible, and long, heavy ocean-rollers break unceasingly upon it.'

nature lovers, as one of the best tourist attractions in South Australia. The absence of predators and any large, permanent human settlement has resulted in a rich variety of wildlife which feels totally unthreatened by the presence of people. Thus, at **Seal Bay**, visitors can walk among the seals. At the western end of the island the 60,000ha (148,000-acre) **Flinders Chase National Park** is home to thousands of species of flora and fauna.

To the east of Kangaroo Island is the **Coorong**, one of South Australia's premier national parks. In 1908, the poet Will Ogilvie wrote of it: 'It is sunset in the Coorong, the ribbon of blue water that divides the ninety mile desert from the sea ... Great flocks of wild-fowl sweep and settle again with strange, discordant cries, and the white beach gleams.'

The northern and western half of South Australia is nothing more than desert. Sand dunes, searing summer temperatures, and scrubby inhospitable terrain have repelled even the most adventurous of explorers.

The Flinders Range is the most extensive mountain range in the state. It stretches 500km (311 miles) from Crystal Brook, just south of Port Pirie to the southern edges of the Lake Eyre Basin. About 650 million years ago the range formed part of the sea bed. Its subsequent uplift has resulted in a series of fossils of sea creatures – trilobites and worms – appearing in the rock formations in the range. These are recognised as the oldest fauna fossils on earth.

The beauty of the ranges, and the establishment of the Flinders Range National Park (1972) and Gammon Ranges National Park (1970), has meant that tourism has become increasingly important. **Wilpena Pound** (a 'pound' is a synclinal basin) is an area of great beauty which has become popular with walkers and explorers.

The **Eyre Peninsula** was the first part of South Australia sighted by Europeans. In 1627 the Dutch explorer Peter Nuyts sighted the peninsula but, deciding not to land, turned back and headed towards Batavia.

The peninsula is sparsely populated and isolated, but the waters of both Spencer Gulf and the Southern Ocean yield a rich harvest of fish, southern rock lobsters, western king prawns, abalone, scallops and Coffin Bay oysters, which are all brought in to Port Lincoln.

At the northern end of the peninsula, **Whyalla** is the centre of the state's steel industry and is one of the most important steel-producing cities in Australia.

The Nullarbor Plain is an arid, scrubby, flat limestone plateau which, when it reaches the Southern Ocean, falls away dramatically in a series of sheer cliffs which tumble as far as 100m (330ft) into the cold seas.

The Nullarbor has the longest straight section of railway track in the world. It is virtually uninhabited. The region experiences less that 250mm (10in) of rainfall per annum, but because of the porous nature of the limestone the rain drains underground so quickly that streams cannot form.

In recent years, both archaeologists and speleologists have found elaborate cave systems under the plain's harsh exterior. The **Mullamullang Cave** in the Madura district is now recognised as the largest cave in Australia. The **Koonalda Cave** contains evidence of Aboriginal habitation dating back 18,000 years.

Below: *The cliffs of the Great Australian Bight lie between Nullarbor and Eucla. There are six clearly marked lookouts. A word of warning: none of the lookout points are for the faint-hearted or for people who can't stand heights. Here the cliffs rise sheer for about 100m (330ft) from the sea, which pounds on the rocks below. There are no safety rails.*

Adelaide and South Australia at a Glance

Sep to **Nov** (spring): Adelaide is noted for the magnificent spring flower displays which grace the large parks and gardens throughout the city. From **Mar** to **May** (autumn) the cool days and changing leaves turn the city's deciduous trees into a magnificent autumn display. During summer the city can become oppressively hot and dry. Many residents leave for the hills or the numerous beach resorts along the coast to the north and south of the city.

Adelaide's **international airport** is 8km (5 miles) west of the city centre. There is a bus service to and from the airport called **JetBus**. Starts early, ends late. For more information toll free 1800 182 160 or www. adelaidemetro.com.au Transit time is usually less than 35 minutes. **Taxis** are readily available and major **car rental** facilities are represented. Best to book ahead if you want a car to meet you.

Adelaide has an integrated **bus** service run by the State Transit Authority. The city centre has a **free bus** service and the **Bee Line Bus Service** operates around the city centre, from King William St to Victoria Square. It operates every 5 minutes from 08:00–18:00. **The Glenelg tram** (a vintage 1929 model) travels regularly

from the city centre to the beachside suburb of Glenelg. It is a delightful trip which includes a short journey through suburban Adelaide. **Trains** are available to the suburbs of Adelaide. For interstate travel the terminal is in **Keswick**, tel: 08 8218 2362, www.trans adelaide.com.au for information and bookings. For the more adventurous the popular Ghan railway runs between Adelaide and Darwin, tel: 1300 736 892, www.gsr.com.au The journey usually takes 23 hours. **Taxi cabs** are readily available in the city, and all hotels and motels have extensive car rental listings.

Adelaide has an extensive selection of accommodation, from five-star hotels in the city centre to popular bed and breakfasts in the suburbs. **Hilton Adelaide**, 233 Victoria Sq, tel: 08 8217 2000, fax: 08 8217 2001. Luxury hotel, central location. **Novotel Adelaide**, Hindley St, tel: 08 8231 5552, fax: 08 8237 3800. Well-located hotel with excellent facilities. **Stamford Plaza Adelaide**, North Terrace, tel: 08 8461 1111, fax: 08 8231 7572. Five-star hotel located in the heart of the city. **Hyatt Regency Adelaide**, Adelaide North Terrace, tel: 08 8231 1234, fax: 08

8931 1120. Adelaide's most elegant hotel, with service and views to match.

BUDGET ACCOMMODATION
Adelaide Regent Apartments, tel: 08 8224 8888, toll free 1800 242 503. Well appointed apartments offering self-catering accommodation. **Festival City Hotel/Motel**, North Terrace, tel: 08 8212 7877, fax: 08 8211 8137. Reasonably priced and central. **City Park Motel**, 471 Pulteney St, tel: 08 8223 1444, fax: 08 8223 1133. Boutique-style motel offers views over South Parklands.

Hahndorf
This German village in the Adelaide hills retains its 19th-century charm. A premier tourist attraction with gift shops, old-world buildings and eating houses all within walking distance. **Hahndorf Inn Motor Lodge**, Main St, tel: 08 8388 1000, fax: 08 8388 1092. Conveniently located for easy exploration. **Hahndorf Molen's Cottage**, Main St, tel: 08 8370 1345, fax: 08 8339 8034. Well-appointed two-bedroom cottage. Walking distance to Hahndorf. **Hahndorf Old Mill**, Main St, tel: 08 8388 7888. Built in 1843, the old mill has been turned into a motel and conference centre.

Adelaide and South Australia at a Glance

Adelaide has recently become one of Australia's most desirable eating destinations. The food is cheap, the local produce is exceptionally high quality and the wines, from the surrounding vineyards in Barossa and Clare Valleys and McLaren Vale, are exceptional. Travellers prepared to explore the Barossa Valley, Clare Valley and Adelaide Hills will also find many world-class eateries. **Hindley Street** is known for its ethnic food while **Gouger Street** has more traditional fair. Check the free booklet, *This Week in Adelaide* (available at most hotels and motels), for up-to-date restaurant listings. An ideal way to sample Adelaide's cuisine is to book into the **Grazing on Gouger** – a hosted progressive luncheon featuring five restaurants with different cuisines. Book on 08 8263 0265. Some of South Australia's best restaurants are located in the easily accessible Adelaide Hills.

The Original Barbecue Inn, Hindley St, tel: 08 8231 3033. Large selection of charcoal-grilled meat and salads.

Adelaide Pavilion, Veale Gardens, tel: 08 8212 7444. Charming garden setting.
Tapas, Hindley St, tel: 08 8211 7446. Fun Spanish restaurant serving a variety of gourmet delights.
Jolley Boathouse, Jolleys Lane, tel: 08 8223 2891. Refurbished boathouse on the Torrens River.
Gouger Fish Restaurant, Gouger St, tel: 08 8231 2320. Award-winning seafood.

Hahndorf

Hahndorf has built its culinary reputation on superb German cooking but the village has many other culinary delights.
Old Mill, 98 Main St, tel: 08 8388 7888. Excellent international cuisine.
German Arms Hotel, 69 Main St, tel: 08 8388 7013. Modern Australian and traditional German cuisine.
Hahndorf Resort-Hans Heysen Restaurant, 145 Main St, tel: 08 8388 7921. Friendly atmosphere, fine dining.

South Australian Visitor & Travel Centre, located at the Torrens River end of King William Street, tel: 1300 65 5276. Conducts a variety of tours. One of the most popular is the Adelaide Heritage Walk.
Adelaide Sightseeing Coach Tours, tel: 08 8231 4144. Offers a comprehensive tour of the city.
Auburn Tours, tel and fax: 08 8564 2144. Tailored personal tour in a vintage car or four-wheel-drive taking in the sites of the Barossa.
Barossa Experience Tours, Tanunda, tel: 08 8563 3248. Comprehensive tours of Barossa Valley and surrounding area at reasonable rates.
Cultural Tourism Professionals, tel: 08 8294 8812, fax 08 8294 8812. Specialising in tours to the state's cultural and desert areas.

The South Australian Government Travel Centre, 18 King William St, tel: 1300 65 5276, open 08:30–17:00.
The Royal Automobile Association of South Australia, Hindmarsh Square, tel: 08 8202 4346, toll free 1800 630 878, www.raa.net An excellent bookshop; provides helpful information and maps.
Suburban Taxi Service, tel: 13 1008.
Cabpay, tel: 08 8227 1123.

ADELAIDE	J	F	M	A	M	J	J	A	S	O	N	D
AVERAGE TEMP. °F	75	75	72	64	59	53	52	53	57	63	68	72
AVERAGE TEMP. °C	24	24	22	18	15	12	11	12	14	17	20	22
SEA TEMP. °F	68	68	66	64	63	61	61	59	59	59	61	66
SEA TEMP. °C	20	20	19	18	17	16	16	15	15	15	16	19
RAINFALL in	1	1	1	2	2.5	3	2.5	2.5	2	2	1	1
RAINFALL mm	20	21	24	44	68	72	67	62	51	44	31	26
Days of Rainfall	4	4	5	9	13	15	16	16	13	11	8	6

8
Perth and
Western Australia

Western Australia, the nation's largest state, is a vast, underpopulated, predominantly desert area like nowhere else in Australia.

It is basically a vast low-lying plateau which rarely rises above 600m (2000ft). The monotonous topography of the state is broken only by the narrow coastal plain which runs down the west coast from Broome to Albany, the low-lying Stirling Range in the south, and the Hamersley Range in the northwest.

Beyond the coastal plain the country degenerates into endless desert. In the centre of the state is the Gibson Desert. In the south the Great Victoria Desert and Nullarbor Plain sprawl across from South Australia. This vast desert wasteland means that, in spite of the state's area, most Western Australians cling to the coast. Less than 15% of the state's population live in rural areas and over 90% live in the fertile South West Land Division which encompasses both Perth and Fremantle.

PERTH

Perth is known for its great charm and beauty. The elegant riverside parks, the network of freeways and the languid beauty of the Swan River all combine to give the city grace and distinction.

Kings Park ★★★

Otherwise known as Mount Eliza, Kings Park is the logical place to start city sightseeing. It offers a superb orientating view of Perth and the graceful Swan River.

Don't Miss

★★★ The Pinnacles: strange shapes surrounded by sand dunes near Jurien, north of Perth.
★★★ Kalbarri National Park: the greatest wildflower display in Australia.
★★★ Monkey Mia: famous for the dolphins.
★★ Wave Rock: near Hyden – an extraordinary wave-shaped rock.
★★ Broome: a tropical town with a fascinating past.
★★ Kalgoorlie: great gold-mining town.

Opposite: *The Manning Gorge in the Kimberley offers cool relief in a dry and harsh landscape.*

Above: *Standing out among the solid Victorian buildings on St Georges Terrace is London Court, a narrow shopping alley notable for its mock Tudor frontages and its models of famous English characters.*

There are a number of interesting brochures on Kings Park. *Guide to Kings Park Botanic Garden* provides a brief history of the gardens and a map identifying the stands of jarrah, karri, tuart and heath in the park. The area has also been planted with flora taken from other 'Mediterranean' climates such as California and South Africa.

London Court ★★

Located on St Georges Terrace, Perth's financial and professional centre, this delightful alley with its mock Tudor frontage buildings is a popular meeting place for people shopping in the Hay Street Pedestrian Mall.

The attractive arcade features models of Dick Whittington, St George and the Dragon, Sir Walter Raleigh and imitations of Big Ben in London and the Grosse Horloge in Rouen.

Barracks Archway ★

Located at the top of St Georges Terrace, Barracks Archway is all that remains of the huge Pensioners' Barracks which once comprised 120 rooms. The arch is nothing more than a hint of the grandeur which once characterised this chequered building, completed in 1863 and used by the Pensioner Guards (retired soldiers) until 1904.

Central Government Precinct ★★

The original heart of Perth is a compact group of 19th-century buildings, close to the site where a tree was felled in 1829 to mark the foundation of the capital. The group of buildings occupies almost an entire city block.

The Central Government Building (1874–1902) has a plaque on its east corner from where all distances are measured. The Perth Town Hall (1867) was built by convict labour. The Deanery (1859) retains its shingle roof. Government House (1864) is surrounded by an English cottage garden.

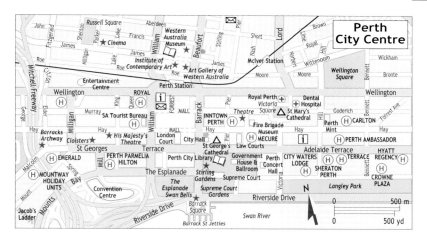

Cloisters ★★

Built in 1858 and located on St Georges Terrace just opposite Mill Street, the Cloisters have been a boys' school, a girls' school, private houses, a training college for clergymen, a university hostel and a café. The Cloisters are now part of the Mount Newman office block.

East Murray Street Precinct ★★

The East Murray Street Precinct, with its large Moreton Bay fig (listed on the National Estate) and its collection of harmonious buildings, is an ideal walk for anyone wanting to recall Perth's glories, when gold had made the state rich.

CITY OF PERTH

Things to do in Perth:
• Investigate the East Murray Street Precinct.
• Board a boat for a trip along the Swan River.
• Spend a day at Rottnest Island.
• Head for Fremantle and wander around its historic precincts.
• Stroll through the city's excellent parks and gardens.
• Explore Perth's many Heritage Trails.
• Try your luck at the Burswood resort casino.

Left: *Perth is the pulse of Western Australia. Its fortunes depend on miners and graziers. In the 1980s, it buzzed with activity and its modern skyline reflects the rapid growth of that period.*

Right: *Rottnest Island provides the ideal 'car-free' getaway for busy Perth residents.*

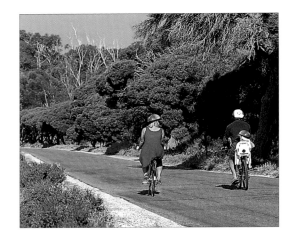

St George's Cathedral ★★

Situated at the corner of St Georges Terrace and Cathedral Avenue, St George's Cathedral was designed by the eminent Australian architect, Edmund Blacket, and built between 1879 and 1888.

Stirling Gardens ★★

Located on the corner of St Georges Terrace and Barrack Street, Stirling Gardens are a wonder to behold in springtime. The blooms and the exquisitely maintained lawns offer a dramatic contrast to the canyons of iron and concrete surrounding the gardens.

St Mary's Cathedral ★★

Located in Victoria Square, this Gothic building was constructed between 1863 and 1865. Among the builders were the Benedictine Monks from Subiaco, who walked to the site every day to help with construction.

This is only a brief summary of the most prominent buildings in this historic city. For those sightseers wanting to investigate the history of Perth and its suburbs, a wide range of Heritage Trail brochures and booklets are available from the National Trust Bookshop in the Old Perth Boys' School building.

ROTTNEST ISLAND

Located 19km (12 miles) off the coast from Perth, **Rottnest Island** is the city's favourite holiday and day tripping destination. Only 12 minutes by air and two hours by water, the island is an accessible location for those wishing to escape from Perth. As recently as the last ice age Rottnest Island was connected to the mainland. The **absence of cars** (everyone on the island rides a bicycle or walks), the historic buildings, the charm of the huge **Moreton Bay figs** and the quiet waters around the island, have been a magnet for Perth people since the 1850s. There are a number of excellent Rottnest Island Heritage Trail walks.

Eating Out

Visitors wanting a good guide to the city's restaurants should refer to *This Week in Perth and Fremantle* which is available free of charge in most hotels.

Beyond Perth

Western Australia's attractions are like those of no other state. The highlights are difficult to access (unless you travel everywhere by air) and involve vast distances. From the south to the north the state has extraordinarily beautiful beaches at **Esperance** (arguably the best in the country), a dramatic shoreline from Albany around to Bunbury, the great karri and jarrah forests of the southwest, the fascinating mining towns of **Kalgoorlie** and **Coolgardie**, the beautiful **Stirling Range National Park**, the historic **Margaret River** area, the coast to the north of Perth with the famous **Shark Bay** and **Monkey Mia** (where dolphins come to the shore), the strange mining towns of the **Pilbara**, the subtropical splendour of **Broome**, the dramatic **Bungle Bungles**, and the wild tropical outback of **Wyndham**, where crocodiles and the mudflats of five converging rivers make for one of the most unusual vistas on the whole continent.

THE GREAT SOUTHERN REGION

The Roaring Forties, blowing across the Indian Ocean, dump their rains on the southern tip of the state, producing a region known for its lush green forests covering its mountain ranges and spreading out into gently undulating valleys.

The area, which enjoys a Mediterranean climate, is also known for its vineyards. In the **Mount Barker** region there are a large number of small, specialist wineries producing high-quality Rhine Rieslings, Chardonnays, Cabernet Sauvignons, Pinot Noirs and Ports.

The centre of the region is **Albany**, a town of 31,000 people which becomes 50,000 in the tourist season. Lying 412km (256 miles) south of Perth, its superb deep-water, land-locked harbour was first discovered by Captain George Vancouver who sailed along the coast in 1791.

VINEYARDS AT MARGARET RIVER

One of the great attractions of Margaret River are the **vineyards** and **wineries.** The climate in the area is perfect for grape growing. The first vines were planted as recently as 1967, but already the produce includes Rhine Riesling, Chardonnay, Semillon, Sauvignon Blanc, Cabernet Sauvignon, Pinot Noir and Shiraz. People wanting to do a little tasting should contact the Margaret River Visitor Centre which has maps and details of opening times. Contact tel: 08 9780 5911.

ESPERANCE

The drive from Esperance west along **Twilight Beach Road** past **West Beach**, **Chapman's Point**, **Blue Haven Beach**, **Salmon Beach**, **Fourth Beach** and **Twilight Beach** is the most beautiful stretch of coastline anywhere in Australia. The white sands, the gently rounded granite cliffs, and the ocean changing from aquamarine near the shore to a deep Prussian blue out near the islands of the Archipelago of the Recherche, is a combination of natural beauties which make Esperance one of the true wonders of the Australian coastline. The sand dunes which have been pushed to fantastic heights by the unforgiving 'Esperance Doctor', are 50–60m (165–197ft) high.

The forests around Albany are home to kookaburras, bush wallabies, kangaroos, emus and parrots. Ranging from forests to coastal wetlands, the region is home to over 3600 of Western Australia's wildflower species.

The beautiful, and appropriately famous, jarrah, karri and tingle trees were the basis for the area's timber industry. As early as 1884, the appropriately named Miller Brothers had established two timber mills at Denmark to the west of Albany. By 1905, most of the accessible timber had been removed and the area became a dairy farming region.

The coastal waters of the region abound with fish, ranging from shark to salmon, flathead, whiting, silver bream, herring and groper.

THE MIDWEST

The area known as 'the midwest' stretches from the ports of Geraldton, Kalbarri and Port Denison right across the state to the edges of civilisation on the perimeters of the Great Victoria Desert. In broad terms, the area divides into three regions – the Batavia Coast, the agricultural heartland, and the Murchison goldfields area.

The **Batavia Coast** was first explored by Dutch sailors who were heading for the great trading port of Batavia in the Dutch East Indies. Crossing the Indian Ocean with the Roaring Forties, they were forced to head due north along the coast of Western Australia.

The economy of the area is primarily agricultural, although in recent times tourism – fuelled by the excellent climate and the variety of historical sites – has grown significantly.

Geraldton, with a population in excess of 30,000, is not only surrounded by sheep grazing, wheat farming and veg-

Below: *Located 586km (364 miles) north of Perth, Kalbarri National Park is noted for its wildflower displays and the spectacular gorges and rock formations cut by the Murchison River.*

etable growing, but is also an important port for the export of grain, mineral sands and gold from the fields in the Murchison area.

To the north of Geraldton is the town of **Kalbarri,** noted for its lobster fishing. The town is on the edge of the Kalbarri National Park, a vast 186,000ha (460,000-acre) sandy park which has some of the best wildflower displays in the country. It is known for its emus, euros, rock wallabies, and red and western grey kangaroos.

Beyond the heartland lies the area of the Murchison goldfields, where the glories of the gold rush in the 1890s have now been overwhelmed by sheep grazing.

Western Australia in the 1880s and 1890s was like Victoria in the 1850s. Men swarmed across the land in a desperate attempt to discover new goldfields. Paddy Hannan's discovery at Kalgoorlie, and the early discoveries at Coolgardie, had sparked true gold fever.

In 1891, the rush to the Murchison goldfields began when Tom Cue discovered gold at the town which now bears his name. In the years that followed, dozens of gold towns grew up only to die when the seams were exhausted and new ones were found elsewhere. Today, the area is a mixture of ghost towns and tiny settlements such as Cue (population 500), Yalgoo (331), Mount Magnet (800) and Sandstone (140).

THE GASCOYNE

In recent years, **Monkey Mia** in the Gascoyne Region has received more attention than most out-of-the-way tourist resorts. This isolated beach at Shark Bay has created international interest because of the remarkable relationship which has developed between visitors and the local dolphin population.

For years it had been common for fishermen to throw the occasional fish to the dolphins. In 1964, a local woman hand-fed one of the dolphins. The dolphins returned the next day and so began a pattern of hand-feeding. Today, this unusual relationship between humans and dolphins has led to the establishment of the **Dolphin Information Centre**.

CUE – A GHOST TOWN

Known as the '**Queen of the Murchison**', Cue is located 650km (405 miles) northeast of Perth. At the turn of the century, Cue was the centre of the **Murchison Goldfields** boasting a population of around 10,000. Now all that is left is a small settlement (current population is around 300) with some of the most grandiose buildings to be seen anywhere in rural Western Australia. Cue's buildings – most notably **The Gentleman's Club**, **The Old Gaol**, the **Government Buildings** and the **Masonic Lodge** – make a walk around the town a fascinating journey into the past. There are also interesting trips to unique **Aboriginal art sites**, the remnants of **Day Dawn** mine, and to the **Red Ochre** mine at Wilgie Mia.

MINING TOWNS IN THE PILBARA

The Pilbara is an area of mines, mining towns and port facilities. The exceptions – **Roebourne**, **Onslow** and **Cossack** – were the earliest towns in the region.

In the last 30 years the four major mining companies – Hamersley Iron, Cliffs Robe River Iron Associates, Goldsworthy Mining Company and Woodside Petroleum – have invested over A\$2 billion establishing major mines at Mount Tom Price, Paraburdoo, Shay Gap, Newman, Pannawonica, and Goldsworthy, constructing 10 new towns, building 1200km (745 miles) of private railways, developing and expanding five ports and completing two pelletising plants.

This fascinating tourist attraction happens to be in Shark Bay where both the first white man and later, the first Englishman, set foot on Australian soil.

On 25 October 1616, **Dirck Hartog** landed at Cape Inscription at the northern tip of Dirk Hartog Island, and in August 1699, **William Dampier**, the famous English adventurer and buccaneer, spent a week charting the shores of the bay. It was Dampier who named the inlet Shark Bay.

THE PILBARA

Containing the largest iron-ore deposits in Australia, the Pilbara starts north of Exmouth, takes in the coastal towns of **Onslow**, **Karratha**, **Dampier**, **Roebourne**, **Cossack**, **Point Sampson**, **Wickham** and **Port Hedland** and runs east through the **Hamersley** and **Ophthalamia ranges** to the edges of the **Great Sandy** and **Gibson deserts**.

The coast experiences blisteringly hot summer weather and monsoonal rains which still produce only an annual average at Onslow of 334mm (13in).

Inland from the coast, nearly all the towns are, or were, company mining towns. The only exceptions (and only because they pre-dated the concept of the company mining town) are **Nullagine** and **Marble Bar**. Both towns grew in the 1890s as a direct result of the discovery of gold in the area.

Marble Bar, once a thriving gold-mining town, is now a tiny settlement of 290 people living in an area widely recognised as the hottest in Australia. The temperature from November to February is consistently over 40°C (104°F) and with only 334mm (13in) annual rainfall, the town experiences a virtual permanent drought.

There is the highly controversial **Wittenoom** where asbestos was once mined. **Newman**, with its 3500 people, was built by the Mount Newman Mining Company as a town for its employees. **Tom Price** was constructed by Hamersley Iron after vast iron-ore reserves were discovered at Mount Tom Price in 1962. **Paraburdoo** was the second of Hamersley Iron's mining towns and **Pannawonica** was built by Robe River Iron Associates.

The mining towns are tiny oases in a vast desert. Were it not for the wealth which lies below the surface it would be unlikely that anyone would want to settle permanently in this inhospitable region.

THE BUNGLE BUNGLES

Known to the local Aborigines as **Purnululu**, the Bungle Bungles are located northeast of Halls Creek – take the Great Northern Highway 109km (68 miles) north from Halls Creek and turn east on the Spring Creek Track – on a road which is so bad that the RAC has this to say about it: 'The distance from the highway to the Three-Ways intersection is only 55km (35 miles), however, the trip will take two or three hours and the track is suitable only for 4WDs with good clearance. Caravans will not survive the trip.' Reaching the campsites involves further travelling for at least another hour. The journey is, however, worth the effort as they are one of the natural wonders of Australia and in 2003 they were placed on the World Heritage List.

Left: *In 1887, the tramway at Cossack in the Pilbara area ran six horse-drawn passenger coaches.*

Above: *Dating back over 350 million years, the Bungle Bungles are formed from sandstone so fine that it crumbles when touched.*

THE KIMBERLEY

This vast area of northwest Western Australia is primarily cattle country. The monsoonal rains that sweep across the region from November to March produce a distinct 'dry' and 'green' season.

Three times the size of England, the Kimberley has over half of its area taken up by only 93 cattle leases. Not surprisingly, it is a region of considerable contrasts. Inland there is the spectacular and unusual beauty of the **Purnululu (Bungle Bungle) National Park**, while on the coast there is the multicultural melting pot of Broome.

The Kimberley is traversed by the Great Northern Highway which runs from Broome to Darwin. **Broome**, with its booming population of 14,436 (2006) which rises to 45,000 between June and August, was once the pearling capital of the world (in 1910 there were over 350 luggers operating out of Broome). Today it is a combination of pearling, tourism, fishing, oil exploration and, in the hinterland, cattle grazing. The area is alive with dangerous animals, in particular, crocodiles. As the tourist brochure explains:

- There is potential danger anywhere saltwater crocodiles occur. If there is any doubt, do not swim, canoe or use small boats in estuaries, tidal rivers, deep pools or mangrove shores.
- Be aware. Keep your eyes open for large crocodiles. Children and pets are at particular risk in the water or at the water's edge.
- Do not paddle, clean fish, prepare food or camp at the water's edge. Fill a bucket with water and do your chores at least five metres away. Returning regularly to the same spot at the water's edge is dangerous.
- Stand at least a few metres back from the water's edge when fishing. Crocodiles have not been known to attack well away from the water.

THE LORD OF BROOME

Although he now has little involvement with Broome, there is no doubt that Lord Alistair McAlpine was responsible for the modern renaissance of this isolated township. A wealthy member of the British aristocracy (and an active memeber of the British Conservative Party during the Thatcher years), he restored and relocated two of the town's most interesting historic buildings – **Matso's Store** and **Captain Gregory's House** and, seeing the potential in the beautiful **Cable Beach** he built a resort of international standards. Today they have all been sold to other interests, but Lord McAlpine's impact on the town is to be seen everywhere.

Left: *Dawn over Broome Harbour captures the tropical splendour of this most isolated town. Once a thriving pearling port, Broome is today a tourist attraction for travellers wanting to experience something far removed from city living.*
Below: *To the north of Fitzroy Crossing in the Kimberley is the Giekie Gorge National Park. Famed for its cool, refreshing waters and its dramatic cliffs, this section also boasts a large population of freshwater crocodiles.*

Apart from crocodiles there are five varieties of pythons, brown snakes and death adders to be found in the region, and fishermen should be wary of stonefish, sea snakes and sharks.

Fitzroy Crossing, a traditional crossing point and resting place, is surrounded by cattle stations. **Halls Creek**, once a gold-mining town with a population of 10,000, is today another service centre for the outlying cattle stations. **Kununurra** was established in 1963 to service the Ord River Irrigation Scheme. While the scheme has been a limited success – 12,000ha (29,000 acres) are now producing peanuts, sunflower seeds, cucumbers, mangos, melons and pawpaws – the area's economy was later enhanced when the Argyle Diamond Mine began production in the early 1980s.

The last town of major importance in Western Australia, and the state's northernmost port, is **Wyndham**. With a population of 900, it acts as a service town for the local cattle stations and various mineral exploration teams. It has become an ideal place for tourists to inspect crocodiles. There is a huge 30m (100ft) long crocodile replica in the town.

Perth and Western Australia at a Glance

BEST TIMES TO VISIT

Sep to **Nov** (spring), to take advantage of the beautiful wildflower displays which Western Australia is justifiably famous for. **Dec** to **Feb**, long, dry, hot summers make beach and water activities a joy on Western Australia's long coastline. The rainfall is so low that every day is almost guaranteed to be sunny. Perth has a warm temperate climate with a short, mild winter and long, dry summers.

GETTING THERE

Perth **International Airport** is 20km (12 miles) northeast of Perth. The **domestic terminal** is 11km (6 miles) northeast of the city.

Bus and **taxi** services are available from both terminals. Transfer time is 30–40 minutes by bus, which stops at the **Airport Bus Service Centre** in the city and at some city hotels and motels. **Car rental** facilities are also available at the airport. Advance reservations are recommended if you wish to have a car at the airport. The famous **Indian-Pacific Railway** operates between Sydney and Perth and passengers can stop at Adelaide and Broken Hill on the route across the continent. The Indian–Pacific is considered to be one of the greatest rail journeys in the world.

GETTING AROUND

CAT buses operate three free city routes – the red, blue and yellow routes. Buses depart every 5–10 minutes between 07:00–18:00 on weekdays. The yellow route circles the city. For more information tel: 13 6213. **Citybus** are the public bus company. They also link to the **ferry service** tickets which are valid for two hours and are used for both bus and ferry. **Trains** operate from Perth to Fremantle, Midland and Armidale.

WHERE TO STAY

Perth has a large variety of hotels and motels ranging from five-star luxury to numerous inexpensive hotels. **Mercure Hotel Perth**, 10 Irwin St, tel: 08 9326 7000, fax: 08 9221 3344. Quality hotel, with modern conveniences. **Hotel Grand Chancellor,** Wellington St, tel: 08 9327 7000, fax: 08 9327 7017. Elegant, well-appointed hotel that offers every luxury. **Perth Parmelia Hilton**, Mill St, tel: 08 9215 2000, fax: 9481 0857. Old-world elegance, in the city centre. **Sheraton Perth**, 207 Adelaide Terrace, tel: 08 9224 7777, fax: 08 9224 7788. Comfortable and convenient. **Mantra**, Hay St, tel: 1300 987 604 or 07 5665 4450. Apartment-style accommodation in this luxury hotel.

BUDGET ACCOMMODATION
Aarons Hotel Perth, Pier St, tel: 08 9325 2133, or 1800 99 8133, fax: 08 9221 2936. Central location. **City Stay Apartments**, 875 Wellington St, tel: 08 9215 1515 or 1800 819 191, fax: 9322 7348. Value for money, central location. **Miss Maud Swedish Hotel**, Murray St, tel: 08 9325 3900, fax: 08 9221 3225. Scandinavian style in the city centre. **Comfort Inn Wentworth Plaza**, Murray St, tel: 08 9338 5000, fax: 08 9321 2443. Comfortable and affordable accommodation.

Fremantle

Historic Fremantle at the mouth of the Swan River is well worth a visit and is easily reached from Perth by train or bus. It has a mixture of beachside atmosphere with great historic interest. **Esplanade Hotel**, cnr Marine Tce & Essex St, tel: 08 9432 4000, fax: 08 9430 4539. International hotel situated in the heart of historic Fremantle. **Tradewinds Hotel Fremantle**, 59 Canning Hwy, tel: 08 9339 8188, fax: 08 9339 2266. Overlooking the Swan River, close to Fremantle.

BUDGET ACCOMMODATION
Henty Executive Apartments, Pakenham St, tel: 08 9279 5915, fax: 08 9279 4390. Good quality serviced apartments.

Perth and Western Australia at a Glance

Perth has an exceptional range of restaurants from traditional European cuisine to all types of Asian and Indian food. Check the free booklet, *This Week in Perth and Fremantle* for up-to-date listings. It is not comprehensive but it offers a good guide to some of the best eateries. It can usually be obtained from tourist offices and large city hotels.

Perugino Restaurant, Outram St, tel: 08 9321 5420. Well located Italian restaurant, exceptional pasta.

Arirang Korean BBQ Restaurant, 91 Barrack St, tel: 08 9225 4855. BBQ eating Korean style; fun and delicious.

Grand Palace Chinese Restaurant, 14 The Esplanade, tel: 08 9221 6333. Traditional Chinese.

Midori Japanese & Korean Restaurant, cnr of Milligan and Wellington Pde, tel: 08 9322 5688. The taste of North Asia with both Japanese and Korean cuisine.

Fraser's Restaurant, Fraser Ave, tel: 08 9481 7100. Beautiful restaurant in Kings Park over-looking the Swan River.

Shun Fung on the River, Old Perth Port, Barrack Square, tel: 08 9221 1868. Exotic flavours served in a stunning location.

Fremantle
Sails Seafood Restaurant, 47 Mews Rd, tel: 08 9430 5050. Famous seafood restaurant, right on the beach.

Capri Restaurant, South Terrace, tel: 08 9335 1399. Centrally located with delightful armosphere.

There is a variety of tours from Perth, ranging from a short trip across to **Rottnest Island** to journeys to the wineries of **Margaret River**, a trip to **Monkey Mia** to see the dolphins, and journeys inland to the historic wheatbelt towns. Rottnest Island, daily ferry from Barrack St jetty. The trip takes two hours. An alternative is the Rottnest Airbus which will get you there in 15 minutes. Check with Perth Visitors Centre, tel: 1300 36 1351.

Stables Yanchep, Yanchep, tel: 08 9561 1606. Exceptional tours offering half-day, full-day and overnight trail rides. Beautiful Yanchep beach and overland treks are a feature. Accommodation and camping make this a truly Australian experience.

Western Xposure, Christian Court, tel: 08 9371 3695, www.westernxposure.com.au Trips to the **Pinnacles** or to **Kalbarri**, **Exmouth** and **Monkey Mia**.

Captain Cook Cruises, tel: 08 9325 3341.

Swan Valley Winery Trails, mobile: 04 1291 7496. Horse-drawn wagons offer a delighful way to see the lovely Swan Valley and visit the wineries. Great for the whole family.

Western Australia Visitor Centre, tel: 1300 36 1351. Has an extensive list of package tours from coach to paddle-steamers. Free information and booking service.

Joy Flights, Royal Aero Club of WA, tel: 08 9581 6222. 30-minute flights over the city and beaches.

Western Australia Visitor Centre, tel: 1300 36 1351. Open 08:30–17:30 weekdays, 09:00–13:00 Saturday.

The Royal Automobile Club of Western Australia, tel: 08 9421 4400.

Budget Rent-A-Car, Perth, toll free: 1300 794 344, www.budget.com.au

PERTH	J	F	M	A	M	J	J	A	S	O	N	D
AVERAGE TEMP. °F	77	79	75	70	63	57	55	57	59	64	68	72
AVERAGE TEMP. °C	25	26	24	21	17	14	13	14	15	18	20	22
SEA TEMP. °F	70	72	70	70	70	68	66	63	63	66	66	68
SEA TEMP. °C	21	22	21	21	21	20	19	17	17	19	19	20
RAINFALL in	0	0.5	1	2	5	8	7	5	3	2	1	0.5
RAINFALL mm	9	12	19	46	123	182	173	135	80	54	22	14
Days of Rainfall	3	3	4	8	14	17	18	17	14	11	7	4

Travel Tips

Tourist Information

There is a vast fund of information about travelling in Australia available from a variety of sources. The Australian Tourist Commission provides good material, free of charge, and is located in major cities abroad, such as London, Chicago, Los Angeles, New York, Toronto, Auckland, Hong Kong, Frankfurt, Tokyo and Singapore, as well as Sydney. Each state and territory has a Tourism Board with its headquarters in the state capital, as well as regional and interstate offices. These will supply maps, brochures and other information on accommodation, transport, tours and restaurants. Usually open 09:00–17:00 on weekdays and on Saturday mornings. The capital city addresses are:

Queensland
The Brisbane Visitor Information Centre, Queen Street Mall, tel: 07 3006 6290.

New South Wales
The Sydney Visitor Information Centre, Darling Harbour, tel: 02 9240 8788.

Australian Capital Territory
The Canberra Visitors Centre, Northbourne Ave, Canberra City, ACT 2601, tel: 02 6205 0044.

Victoria – RACV Travel Centre, 123 Queen Street, Melbourne, Victoria 3000, tel: 13 1329.

Tasmania – Tasmanian Travel Centre, cnr Elizabeth and Davey St, Hobart 7000, tel: 1800 990 440 or 03 6238 4222.

South Australia – South Australian Travel Centre, 18 King William St, Adelaide SA 5000, tel: 08 8303 2220.

Western Australia – Tourism Western Australia, Forest Place, Perth WA 6000, tel: 1300 361 351 or 08 9483 1111.

Northern Territory – Tourism Top End, 6 Bennett Street, Darwin, NT 0800, tel: 1300 138 886

Most cities and towns have at least one information centre with details of local sights and booking facilities for accommodation and local tours. Remember, however, that many have links with the services they advocate and may not be strictly impartial. The visitor centres and offices of the National Parks and Wildlife Service provide useful material for areas under its jurisdiction, and the National Trust offers free walking tour guides from its offices or, often, from local tourist centres. Other useful sources are the motoring organisations which provide excellent free maps for members of affiliated organisations. Their addresses are:

Queensland – RACQ, GPO Building 261, Queen Street, Qld 4006, tel: 1800 629 501, www.racq.com.au

New South Wales
NRMA, 74–76 King Street, Sydney, NSW 2000, tel: 1300 13 11 22, www.mynrma.com.au

Victoria – RACV, 360 Bourke Street, Melbourne, Victoria 3000, tel: 13 1329, www.racv.com.au

Tasmania – RACT, corner Patrick and Murray Streets, Hobart, Tasmania 7000, tel: 03 6232 6300 or toll free: 13 2722, www.ract.com.au

South Australia – RAA,

41 Hindmarsh Square,
Adelaide, SA 5000,
tel: 08 8202 4589,
www.raa.net
Western Australia – RAC,
228 Adelaide Terrace, Perth,
WA 6000, tel: 13 1703,
www.rac.com.au
Northern Territory
Automobile Association of
the Northern Territory, 79–81
Smith Street,Darwin, NT
0800, tel: 08 8981 3837,
www.aant.com.au
For information on various
tours and tour operators,
contact the outlets listed
in this section.

Entry Requirements

To enter Australia a valid
passport is required and,
unless you are a New
Zealander, you will need a
visa. This can be obtained in
advance from an Australian
consular office abroad. You
can apply for a short term
holiday visa on line. This is
called an ETA (Electronic
Travel Authority). Check out
www.migrationint.com.au
This website will answer all
your questions. Holiday and
visiting visas will allow you up
to three months in Australia.
The cost is A$20. Extensions
requested from within
Australia can be costly.
Furthermore, the amount of
time you plan to spend in the
country is not entirely at your
own discretion. Embassy
officials might limit your time if
you appear unsavoury in their
eyes. A return ticket and 'sufficient funds' are also required,
although the meaning of the
latter is clearly debatable.

A Working Holiday-Maker
visa exists for 'young' people
(usually meaning 18 to 26)
from Ireland, the Netherlands,
the UK, Canada and Japan,
Germany, Republic of Korea
and Malta. The visa is available from the country of
origin, valid for up to one
year costs A$69. It permits
casual employment only.
Most countries now offer
short-term travellers visas via
Electroni Travel Authority or
ETA from travel agents. There
are no fees or stamps. The
visa is for three months and
has multiple entry. It permits
casual rather than full-time
employment. Fruit-picking is
one of the most common,
short-term job prospects.
Long stay visitor's visa is for
between three to six months.
Most short stay visas cost
A$20. You can apply on line
for an extension to your visa.
If you want to apply for a
longer visa or extend your
visa you must apply to the
Department of Immigration
and Multicultural and
Indigenous Affairs (DIMIA)
This information can
be accessed on www.
migrationint.com.au
Visa extensions can take a
long time and cost A$70,
which must be paid upfront
and will not be refunded,
regardless of the outcome.

Air Travel

Australia is a popular destination so be sure to book
well in advance, particularly
if you wish to travel at major
holiday times or via popular
routes. Prices vary greatly

depending on whether you
deal with an airline or agent,
the route you choose, the time
of year etc., so shop around.
Remember that some flights
may be cheap for a good
reason, entailing several stops
and a long, uncomfortable
journey. Townsville, Cairns,
Darwin and all state capitals
with the exception of Hobart
have direct air links with
overseas destinations (Port
Hedland has flights to and
from Bali), which creates the
possibility of arriving and
departing from different
Australian cities. Visitors
should recognise that Sydney
(Kingsford Smith) airport is the
country's major air terminal
and this can mean delays with
landing and customs. An airport bus service usually exists
to transport you into the city.
Departure taxes are included
in the cost of all airline tickets.
Domestic air travel is strictly
non-smoking.
For those who prefer the idea
of travelling by sea, **P&O**,
Cunard and the **Princess Line**
still offer ocean cruises to
Australia, albeit at a price.

Road Travel

The vast distances of
Australia, and the lack of
public transport in places
like Alice Springs, can make
car rental attractive if you are
tired of tours. The airports,
cities and towns of Australia
offer the visitor a large number of car rental agencies,
both local and international.
This competition means a
range of prices and plenty
of temporary specials, so

investigate the options. The major companies – **Avis**, **Hertz** and **Budget** – dominate the airports. They differ little on typical round-the-city rentals, but special offers emerge with less typical and longer-term deals. While unlimited kilometre rates are normal around the city, country and remote driving can incur a higher flat rate plus a kilometre charge. And don't forget insurance cover. Smaller companies are often cheaper, but certainly not always, even if they appear so at first. Be sure to read the fine print and weigh up the pros and cons. A valid driving licence is, of course, essential when hiring a car and applicants usually must be over 21. One-way rentals between major cities are available but are not very economical. Note that smaller cars may be cheaper but are not as comfortable on a long journey. Restrictions may also apply with regard to crossing state boundaries and, depending on the type of car you rent, concerning driving on unsealed roads. A four-wheel-drive could be a wise choice for outback driving or a campervan for long distances.

Clothes: What to Pack

Australia enjoys long hot summers and generally mild winters. People dress informally, though 'smart casual' wear is often required after dark at theatres and other art/entertainment venues, and by the more sophisticated hotels and restaurants. Beach wear is acceptable only on the beach and in beach fast food and casual eateries; casual clothing is customary in most places. For summer months (October to April), pack lightweight garments, a hat, and plenty of sunscreen. For travellers with very fair skin, a sun protection factor (SPF) of 15+ is the minimum. Remember, Australia has the highest rate of skin cancer in the world, and suffering from sunstroke, painful or peeling skin is a high price to pay for a 'golden' tan.

It can get cool at night. Most of the east coast experiences summer rains. Bring an umbrella. In winter, only Melbourne and Canberra get really cold.

Money Matters

Bank hours are usually 09:00–16:00, Monday–Thursday with an extension until 17:00 on Fridays, although, in some major cities, hours can be 08:00–16:00 Monday–Friday. Building societies are often open longer than banks. Traveller's cheques are most readily dealt with, particularly if made out in Australian dollars, and typically receive a better exchange rate than foreign currency. However, virtually all banks will readily and efficiently change both, albeit with varying charges. A passport is usually sufficient proof of identity. Credit cards are widely in use and preferred by car rental agencies but may not be so welcome in remote areas or smaller shops.

In Australia, there are 100 cents to the dollar. Coins come in 5c, 10c, 20c, 50c, A$1 and A$2 denominations and there are A$5, A$10, A$20, A$50 and A$100 notes. Any quantity of money can be taken in and out of the country, although, for amounts over A$5000 you must complete a form. If staying for any duration you could open a cashcard account with a major bank, allowing you access to automatic teller machines (ATMs), which are very widespread and open 24 hours. The cashcards permit you to withdraw A$400 to A$500 a day and can be used to make calls in special phone booths distributed throughout the country. They are also linked to the 'EFTPOS' system (Electronic Funds Transfer at the Point of Sale) which allows you to pay for goods and services in some stores.

Tipping

Tipping is not standard practice in Australia. You may wish to add an extra 10% to the bill at a restaurant if you are impressed with the service, but it is not mandatory. Restaurant prices carry an extra 10% Goods and Service Tax. The food in Australia is plentiful, high quality and cheap, although manufactured goods tend to be more expensive. Waiting staff are paid the standard Australian minimum wage, so they are not dependent on tips, unlike their counterparts in other countries.

Trading Hours

These are from 08:30 or 09:00 until 17:00 or 17:30, Monday–Friday and 09:00–16:00 on Saturday, with late-night shopping on Thursday and/or Friday, when the shops close at 20:00 or 21:00. However, these hours vary somewhat in different centres. Major retailers stay open until 16:00 on a Saturday and most are open on Sundays. Major supermarket chains now tend to open seven days a week in more densely populated areas. Corner shops, milk bars, delis (the common term for delicatessens) and city bookshops also open for extended trading.

Accommodation

There is a truly comprehensive guide to accommodation in Australia which covers all levels of hotels, motels, guest houses and rented accommodation. It is a joint production of the RACV (the Victorian road association) and the RAASA (the South Australian road association). Titled *A–Z Australian Accommodation Guide,* it is published regularly and can be purchased from any state road association outlet. It is very detailed, providing star ratings as well as up-to-date information about prices and facilities. Anyone intending to stay in Australia for an extended period should purchase this excellent publication. No commercial publications can compete with it.

Electricity Supply

The electrical current in Australia is 220–240 volts AC. The local plug-and-socket system uses three pins. These are not the same as those utilised in the UK and only upmarket hotels and motels tend to have appropriate converters. Decent hardware stores may carry adaptors but, failing this, an Australian plug can usually be fitted to an electrical applicance from abroad.

Health and Personal Safety

Australia is a country with high standards of hygiene and very safe food and drinking water. As a result, special precautions are not necessary. No vaccinations are required unless some time has been spent in an infected country in the previous two weeks, although immunisation is always a good idea if your international itinerary is broad.

The intense sun, however, could be a problem, particularly for visitors from more temperate climates. Australia has a high skin cancer rate so be sure, if spending any length of time in its glare, to apply sun cream, wear a broad-brimmed hat, and a shirt with a collar and preferably long sleeves. Australia offers free service at public hospitals to its own citizens and permanent residents, and has universal health care under the Medicare system. This covers either most or all of the cost of visiting a general practitioner, depending largely on whether bulk-billing practices are utilised. However, these services only extend to citizens of the United Kingdom and New Zealand. All visitors will have to pay in full and upfront for dental treatment, ambulance charges and medicines. The cost of an unsubsidised, standard visit to a doctor is currently around A$35–A$45 but remember that serious problems can become expensive. Travel insurance covering medical care and medicines is therefore recommended. A personal basic medical kit would also be a good idea. The telephone number for emergencies is 000, and both crisis hotlines and interpreter services are at the front of the White Pages in the telephone directory. Note that condoms are available at chemists, some all-night stores and at vending machines in the toilets of universities and some hotels. The pill is only available on prescription and so requires a visit to a doctor.

Health Hazards

When bushwalking be sure to wear boots, thick long socks

and long trousers, and be careful where you put your hands. Ticks and leeches are common in the scrub so check your body thoroughly after bushwalking as ticks can be dangerous if unnoticed. Ticks can be removed with kerosene or methylated spirits (don't break the head off inside your body) and leeches with salt or heat. The chances of being attacked, stung or bitten by venomous wildlife are extremely remote but, if a poisonous snake or spider should bite, try to catch the offending creature as antivenenes are available, but don't risk another bite in the process. Stay calm, wrap the area in a tight bandage, as you would with a sprained ankle (DON'T use a tourniquet or suck out the poison), attach a splint to the limb, keep very still and send for medical help. A similar procedure applies to poisons incurred from marine life. Sea wasps are a deadly type of jellyfish which sting with their tentacles, causing telltale welt marks. Douse the wound with vinegar and don't remove the stingers. Always wear hard-soled boots if walking on a reef because of sharp corals and poisonous cone shells and stonefish.

If travelling in the outback it is important to drive very carefully. Some roads are not well developed and the behaviour of other drivers is always of concern. If a huge truck (a road train) comes along, get out of the way as they most certainly won't make way for you.

Respect fire bans (broadcast on the radio) and be careful with cigarette butts and broken glass which can ignite bushfires in hot, dry weather. If caught in a fire, head for a clearing (avoid dense tree growth). Get off the road, stay in the vehicle, get under the dashboard and cover yourself, preferably with a woollen blanket.

If bushwalking or camping be sure to leave an itinerary with friends and go carefully prepared. Remember that nights can turn out to be freezing despite the day-time temperature.

Emergency

The national number for all emergencies is 000. This will get you connected to police, ambulance or other emergency services. All telephone directories have extensive listings of emergency services and facilities in the front section of the book.

CONVERSION CHART

FROM	TO	MULTIPLY BY
Centimetres	inches	0.394
Inches	centimetres	2.54
Metres	feet	3.28
Feet	metres	0.305
Metres	yards	1.09
Yards	metres	0.914
Kilometres	miles	0.621
Miles	kilometres	1.61
Grams	ounces	0.035
Ounces	grams	28.3
Kilograms	pounds	2.20
Pounds	kilograms	0.454
Tonnes	tons	0.984
Tons	tonnes	1.02
Hectares	acres	2.47
Acres	hectares	0.405
Square kilometres	square miles	0.386
Square miles	square kilometres	2.59
Millilitres	fluid ounces	0.0352
Fluid ounces	millilitres	28.4
Litres	pints	1.76
Pints	litres	0.568
Kilometres	miles	0.621
Miles	kilometres	1.61

To convert Celsius to Fahrenheit: 1.8 x degrees Celsius + 32
To convert Fahrenheit to Celsius: 0.5555 x degrees Fahrenheit – 32

INDEX

Page numbers in **bold** refer to photographs.